Project Manager's Spotlight on

Risk Management

About the Author

Kim Heldman is the Chief Information Officer for the Colorado Department of Natural Resources. She has more than 14 years of project management experience in the information technology field. She has managed small, medium, and large projects over the course of her career and shares her breadth of experience and knowledge in her books through examples, stories, and tips.

Kim Heldman is the author of several other project management books, including *PMP Final Exam Review, Project Management JumpStart,* and the top-selling *PMP: Project Management Professional Study Guide*, all from Sybex. You can learn more about Kim at her website: www.KimHeldman.com.

Project Manager's Spotlight on

Risk Management

KIM HELDMAN

JOSSEY-BASS
A Wiley Imprint
www.josseybass.com

Library of Congress Card Number: 2005920769

ISBN: 0-7821-4411-X

Jossey-Bass books and products are available through most bookstores. To contact Jossey-Bass directly call our Customer Care Department within the U.S. at 800-956-7739, outside the U.S. at 317-572-3986, or fax 317-572-4002.

Jossey-Bass also publishes its books in a variety of electronic formats. Some content that appears in print may not be available in electronic books.

Publisher: Neil Edde
Acquisitions Editor: Heather O'Connor
Developmental Editor: Jeff Kellum
Production Editor: Leslie E.H. Light
Technical Editor: Chance Reichel
Copyeditor: Kim Wimpsett
Compositor: Maureen Forys, Happenstance Type-O-Rama
Graphic Illustrator: Happenstance Type-O-Rama
Proofreaders: Nancy Riddiough, Candace English, Jim Brook
Indexer: Ted Laux
Book Designer: Maureen Forys, Happenstance Type-O-Rama
Cover Designer and Illustrator: Daniel Ziegler, Ziegler Design

Printed in the United States of America
FIRST EDITION
PB Printing   10 9 8 7 6 5 4 3

For BB, the biggest risk I ever took.

Kimmie

Contents

Foreword

The Project Manager's Spotlight Series is written for those of you who are engaged in projects at the day-to-day level of business. You're working on projects such as server consolidation, piloting new products in the marketplace, or opening a new branch or storefront. These day-to-day projects keep businesses moving forward, carving out market share, meeting strategic goals, and improving the firm's bottom line. These projects, while vitally important to the companies you work for, are not necessarily multi-million dollar, multi-year projects that require meticulous disciplines and precise methodologies.

The Project Manager's Spotlight Series shows you the how-to's of project management on a practical level. These books help you apply solid principles of project management without the rigor. You'll find tools, tips, and techniques to help you use Project Management Institute–based practices in your small- to medium-sized projects; these are tips you can read over the weekend and be ready and able to apply on Monday morning.

—Kim Heldman

Acknowledgments

There are so many people to thank for their help with this project, I'm not sure where to begin. I think I'll start with Heather O'Connor, the acquisitions editor for this book and the first person I shared the Spotlight Series idea with. She took the idea and ran with it and was instrumental in getting this series off the ground. She also was very gracious and helpful with her comments on both the series idea and this manuscript. Thank you, Heather. This series wouldn't have been possible without your belief in it and your hard work to bring it to reality.

Thank you, as always, to Neil Edde, Publisher. Way back when, he took a chance on me and got me started on this crazy notion that I could write a book. I never would have believed it without the encouragement and support from Neil and his staff. He also went to bat for this series and again, thanks Neil, for the opportunity to write this book, launch this series, and work with your incredible, dedicated staff.

Jeff Kellum took over as developmental editor when Heather went on leave. Jeff has been great to work with and has had many helpful suggestions along the way. He said he enjoyed reading this book which was a great encouragement to me. Thank you, Jeff, for your help and support.

Thank you to Chance Reichel, who worked as the technical editor for this book. He did a great job of pointing out information and tips that would make the text stronger. I really appreciate his help.

It's amazing how many folks are involved in creating a book. Without each of them and their expertise, the final product wouldn't be what you're seeing here. Sometimes I think the writing is the easy part and these folks have the difficult part—making suggestions and corrections and asking me what I was thinking in rough parts of the manuscript. Thank you to each of you for your expertise and suggestions. Leslie Light, production editor, has been terrific at keeping us all on schedule. Kim Wimpsett, copyeditor, asked a lot of those "what are you thinking" questions, only she was very professional about it and every time those questions helped me improve the text. Thank you as well to the behind-the-scenes crew at Sybex: Maureen Forys and the compositors at Happenstance Type-O-Rama, the proofreaders, and always, the indexer, Ted Laux.

Last but never least, thank you to my husband, BB, for your love, encouragement, and support. Thanks for believing in me and for the many dinners you served me in front of the computer screen while I was writing away.

Introduction

*P*roject Manager's Spotlight on Risk Management was written for those of you who want to know more about project risk and how to take advantage of the opportunities risk presents or about how to reduce or eliminate the impact it has on your project.

This book explores risks and risk management from a practical, hands-on approach. It will equip you with questions to ask, tools and techniques to implement, checklists to use, and templates to apply to your projects immediately.

This book has a lot of examples of the types of risks that can plague your project. Reading this book will help you identify risks on projects that you may not have thought of before. It will walk you through how to identify those risks and what to do about them should they occur.

Reading this book will give you a solid foundation in risk management practices. From here, you can build on this knowledge by taking project management classes, reading other books in this series or on this topic, and networking with others in your organization. This book is based on the project management guidelines recommended by the Project Management Institute (PMI), and many of the terms, concepts, and processes you'll read about in this book are based on the PMI publication *A Guide to the Project Management Body of Knowledge (PMBOK Guide)*. This book assumes you have some hands-on project management experience and some familiarity with project management terms and processes as described in *A Guide to the PMBOK*. For those of you who need a refresher, Appendix A describes the nine Knowledge Areas found in *A Guide to the PMBOK* and the five project management processes.

Who Should Read This Book?

If you're serious about increasing your chances for an on-time, on-budget project, you should read this book. Risk management is a process that should be required for all projects, no matter how big or how small. Sometimes simply having an understanding of what's lurking around the corner is enough to reduce the threat of a schedule delay or a budget overrun. This book will walk you through the steps of identifying risks, prioritizing them, deciding which risks require a response plan to deal with them should they occur, monitoring the project for new risks, and evaluating the overall risk strategy so your next project benefits from what you learned about this project.

Those of you who are experienced at project management will find this book beneficial because you can combine what you know from practice with the additional tips and processes outlined here, making your risk management strategy more effective than ever. Those of you who don't have a lot of hands on experience in project management will benefit from this book as well. I'll step you through exactly what you should do to discover risks and how to deal with them.

The Spotlight Series

The Spotlight Series is designed to give you practical, real-life information on specific project management topics such as risk, project planning, and change management. Many times, the theory of these processes makes sense when you're reading about them, but when it's time to implement, you're left scratching your head wondering exactly how to go about it. The books in this series are intended to help you put project processes and methodologies into place on your next project without any guesswork. The authors of this series have worked hard to anticipate the kinds of questions project managers might ask and to explain their topics in a step-by-step approach so you can put what you're reading into practice.

If you find that the topic of project management interests you, I strongly recommend you consider becoming a certified Project Management Professional (PMP) through the PMI. This is the de facto standard in project management methodologies. You'll find many organizations now require a PMP certification for project management jobs. For more information on this topic and to help prepare you for this exam, read my *PMP Project Management Professional Study Guide* from Sybex.

CHAPTER 1

What Is Risk Management?

Can you name the ultimate project management four-letter word? You guessed it: R-I-S-K. This word is uttered either in complete confidence or under the breath as something the project manager wished he or she knew something more about.

Risk management is an integral part of project management. I'll start this chapter with a discussion of the basics of risk management, including the definition of risk, the purposes of risk management, the processes involved with risk management, and principles of risk management.

At the conclusion of this chapter, I'll introduce a case study that you can follow throughout the book. The project manager in the case study will handle issues in her project that I've discussed during the chapter. Don't be caught off guard if there are a few surprises along the way. After all, that's how most projects work.

Are you ready to dive in?

Defining Risk

Most of us tend to think of *risk* in terms of negative consequences. It's true that risks are potential events that pose threats to the project. But they're also potential opportunities. That's the side of the equation we often forget.

For instance, did you know you're taking a risk by reading this book? You're investing a few hours of your time reading about the topic of risk and risk management—and for that I thank you—but it's time that you can't regain once you expend it. You will (I hope) get to the end of this book and realize you learned a lot more about risk than what you knew before you started. In that case, you've taken on a risk and benefited from it. The risk (the threat of a loss of time that you can't regain) will thus end in opportunity because you'll have achieved something at the conclusion of the activity that you didn't have in the beginning.

NOTE   Risks are like exercise: no pain, no gain. Accomplishment is rarely possible without taking risks.

Likewise, you take other risks in your daily routine of which you probably aren't consciously aware. Perhaps you cross a busy intersection on the way from the bus stop to your office. You wait for the walk sign, look both ways before stepping out onto the curb, and proceed to the other side. But let's say you're late for a meeting with the big boss. You can stand on the corner and wait for the walk light, making you even later for the meeting, or you can cross against the light once the traffic has cleared. You weigh the consequences of both actions and decide to walk against traffic.

Chances are you probably didn't consciously perform a complete analysis of all the risks and their consequences involved in these two scenarios before reaching a decision. You likely made a snap judgment in both cases. In the first example, you picked up this book and thought you'd learn something by reading it, so you purchased a copy. In the second, you weighed the probability of getting hit by a car against the likelihood of getting yelled at by the big boss for being late. Even though the consequences of getting hit by a car have significantly more impact, you decided that being yelled at was a more likely outcome and chose to avoid this risk by taking on the other.

Organizations and individuals make decisions regarding project risks every day. They might use a formally recognized, documented process or go with the "fly-by-the-seat-of-your-pants" approach. I hope after reading this book you won't exercise snap judgment about project risks anymore but will instead develop a sound methodology for identifying, analyzing, prioritizing, and planning for risks.

Project Risk

All projects begin with goals. The point of the project is to meet and satisfy the goals the stakeholders agreed on when the project was undertaken. Risk is what prevents you from meeting those goals. (What? Your stakeholders didn't agree on the goals? We'll talk more about that in Chapter 4, "Preventing Scope and Schedule Risks.")

NOTE   This may come as a surprise to all you eternal optimists out there, but all projects have risks. Unfortunately, covering your eyes and saying "you can't see me" doesn't make them go away.

As I stated earlier, most organizations, and most individuals, really, think about risks in terms of harm or danger. What's at stake, how much could we lose, and how bad will it hurt? are the initial questions that surface when we think about risk. I don't mean to be a downer—but I'll spend the majority of this book discussing risks from the perspective of the threats they pose to the project (and their consequences), because after all, unidentified and unplanned for risks are project killers. Chances are you've experienced a failed project or two as a result of unidentified or unplanned risks. As you progress through the book, I'll discuss techniques that lower or eliminate the consequences of risk and thus give your projects a head start to success.

Organizations and Project Risk

Executive managers are responsible for making decisions that benefit the corporation, the shareholders, the constituents, and the others they represent. Whether it is a for-profit company, a governmental organization, a not-for-profit organization, an education-focused business, and so on, the executives at the top have one goal in mind—maximize benefits to the organization and to their shareholders (all the while making themselves look good for future promotional purposes, but that's another book). To do that, the company must minimize bad risks while maximizing the opportunities that good risks may present. This is where you come in.

For executives to make good decisions, they need information. Risk identification and analysis is a part of the vital information they'll use when determining a go or no-go decision regarding the project. And you are the one responsible for reporting on the risks and their potential impacts to the executives to assist them in their decision-making process.

Risk management, unfortunately, is probably one of the most often skipped project management knowledge areas on small-to-medium-sized projects. Many project managers I know take the attitude that they'll deal with the risks when and if they occur rather than take the time to identify and plan for them before beginning the work of the project.

On a small project, even just an hour or two of time spent on risk management can mean the difference between project success and project failure. The information you learn doing simple risk analysis could prove invaluable to your organization. I can't guarantee you project success, but I can guarantee you a much higher potential for project failure if you don't practice basic risk management techniques and inform your executives of the potential for bad juju before it hits.

Applying the risk management processes you'll learn about in this book will help you manage successful projects that improve your organization's performance, profits, efficiency, and market share; provide better market presence; and meet the organization's goals.

The Spotlight Series is geared toward those of you who manage small-to-medium-sized projects. You and I are the ones out there keeping the everyday business functions forging ahead with the small-to-medium-sized projects such as consolidating servers, launching websites, conducting space planning, implementing new purchasing procedures, and so on.

You may be asking, "What does *small* mean?" Well, the answer is relative. A small project with minimal impact to one organization could be huge with devastating impacts to another. For example, your $50,000 project in an organization that generates $500 million a year in revenues is relatively harmless to the bottom line if the project should fail. Conversely, the failure of a $50,000 project to a small business owner could send her into bankruptcy. A small business owner likely couldn't afford the impact of even one risk consequence whereas the large organization could easily invest twice the original amount of the project without batting an eye. Therefore, the risk to the organization is relative as well. (Don't fool yourself, though; you'll have to report to someone about why the original $50,000 wasn't enough. The risk in this case rests with you. Did you plan the project appropriately? Did you estimate activities and budget accurately? And did you identify and plan safe, client-approved strategies for managing risks that could have caused the need for more project funds?)

Remember that your success with small projects will win you larger and larger project assignments. One way to assure you get those juicy assignments is not skipping the risk management processes.

Your company takes on risk with every project the executive team approves. They supply resources, time, money, and sometimes even stake their reputations on projects. Those same resources could be applied to other projects. But the decision makers weigh the possible outcomes of your project over another and decide to run with the project you're assigned. When projects are approved, the benefit, or perceived opportunity, outweighs the perceived threat of *not* completing the project. When the opposite is true, the project never sees the light of day.

NOTE   Most organizations (and individuals) will take risks when the risk benefits outweigh the consequences of an undesirable outcome.

You may be scratching your head right now wondering why the co-worker downwind from you got his project approved while yours was nixed for no apparent reason. Many things can come into play in decisions such as this, including power plays (someone somewhere doesn't like someone else who may benefit from the project), the executive in charge doesn't like the project, favoritism, and other similar office politics. More apparent reasons might play a part as well, such as the project isn't in keeping with the company's mission, no money exists for the project, enough resources aren't available to apply to the project, the risks outweigh the benefits, and so on. I'm certain you can come up with as many reasons as I can.

As you explore risks and consequences and their impact on the organization through the course of this book, keep in mind that executives sometimes seem to defy logical reason when making decisions. They choose projects that have risks with potentially devastating consequences to the organization while brushing off other projects that to us seem like a no-brainer. So when you're wondering about why your project wasn't approved—my advice is don't. Move on to your next assignment and apply solid project management and risk management techniques to help assure its success.

Purpose of Risk Management

The good news is risk isn't the enemy. The bad news is the consequences of ignoring risk can be. What you don't know can hurt you when it comes to risk. The goal of risk management is identifying potential risks, analyzing risks to determine those that have the greatest probability of occurring, identifying the risks that have the greatest impact on the project if they should occur, and defining plans that help mitigate or lessen the risk's impact or avoid the risks while making the most of opportunity.

Project management means applying skills, knowledge, and established project management tools and techniques to your projects to produce the best results possible while meeting stakeholder expectations.

Risk management means applying skills, knowledge, and risk management tools and techniques to your projects to reduce threats to an acceptable level while maximizing opportunities.

More specifically, risk management concerns these five areas:

- Identifying and documenting risks
- Analyzing and prioritizing risks
- Performing risk planning

- Monitoring risk plans and applying controls
- Performing risk audits and reviews

I'll describe each of these processes in further detail in their own chapters, so in this section I'll stick with a high-level definition for each. These processes are highly interactive, and to understand how they all work together, you'll first look at the purpose for each.

Identifying and documenting risks This one is fairly straightforward. The first step of your risk management approach is identifying and writing down all the potential risks that exist on your project. It doesn't stop there, however. Identifying risks occurs throughout the life of the project. Every life-cycle phase brings its own challenges and opportunities, which means more opportunity for project risk.

Analyzing and prioritizing risks These processes are a little more complicated. Now that you know what the risks are, you'll apply tools and techniques to determine which ones have the greatest potential for harm (and for good) to the project. The analyzing and prioritizing process determines which risks require plans.

Performing risk planning Risk planning concerns developing strategies that document how you'll deal with the risks if they occur. Not all risks require response plans. You may choose to live with the consequences of a risk event if it occurs.

Monitoring risk plans and applying controls This process involves evaluating the risk response plans you've put into action and implementing any corrections needed to make certain the plan is effective and the risks are handled appropriately and timely.

Performing risk audits and reviews This process is different from the previous one because it's performed after the project is completed. Monitoring risks occurs throughout the life of the project. Performing a risk audit is a lot like documenting lessons learned. You'll document information as the project progresses, but the risk audit analysis is performed at the end of the project.

Iterative Process

You can see from the discussion in the previous section how the risk management processes interact. Once the project manager (or project team) identifies a risk, she analyzes it to determine its potential impact on the project. Then she develops a plan that outlines how to deal with the impacts of the risk should they occur, and monitors, tracks, and perhaps changes the plan as a result of new information. This means she may identify new risks, requiring more plans, and so on.

Risk management, just like project management, is an iterative process, and effective communication is at its core. Without communication and constructive information exchange between key stakeholders, project team members, management, the project sponsor, and so on, risk management wouldn't work well. The same is true for the project management processes.

The following illustration shows the iterative nature of risk management and the interaction between its processes.

Risk management is tightly integrated with the project management processes and, like project management itself, is not a one-time process. To illustrate this point, the next illustration shows the project life-cycle processes (in italics in the graphic) plotted with the risk management processes to demonstrate how closely linked they are. (Appendix A contains a refresher on the project management life-cycle processes if you need a review.)

Probability and Impact

I've already touched on two topics that need a little further explanation before you proceed—probability and impact. You'll spend a great deal of time with these subjects in Chapter 5, "Analyzing and Prioritizing Risks," but for now some explanations are in order.

Probability is simply the likelihood that a risk event will occur. Let's say you're busy planning the annual St. Patrick's Day parade. The weather forecasters say today has a 20 percent chance of rain. Therefore, the probability it will rain on your parade is 20 percent.

Risk *impact* is the result of the probability of the risk event occurring plus the consequences of the risk event. Impact, in laymen's terms, tells you how bad or how good the realized risk is going to hurt.

Back to the rain example. Perhaps your organization has invested $75,000 in a float scheduled to appear in the parade's third position. This is a prime spot because folks watching the parade are still energized and watching the events closely. This means the advertising panel on the side of the float with your organization's name in huge letters is going to get a lot of visibility. This translates, you hope, into more business. However, if it rains, the impact to the organization is the $75,000 (at a minimum) invested in the float. The potential loss of business is also an impact of this risk event and could be added to the $75,000 to determine a total financial impact. So how bad will it hurt if it rains? The cost is $75,000 plus the loss of business and other time or resources expended preparing the float, assuming a total washout.

Propensity for Risk

The propensity for project risk depends on the project's life-cycle phase. Risks are most likely to occur during the Initiating phase and least likely to occur during the Closing phase. Don't let this fool you though: risks can occur at any time during the course of the project. Intuitively, it makes a lot of sense that risks have a greater chance of occurring earlier in the project. The beginning of the project has lots of uncertainty. Cost-benefit analyses are being performed, resources are being identified but may not be available, market forces may cause a shift in focus, and so on. Many events can happen early on that increase project risk (including the risk of the project getting killed for a host of reasons), so the probability for risk is greatest in the early phases. As you approach the closing phase, the majority of the project work is completed, so the probability of risk events occurring decreases. Chances are a few risks will occur along the way, but I know you have great plans in place to handle them.

You can see the relationship of risks and their probability across the project life-cycle processes in the following graphic.

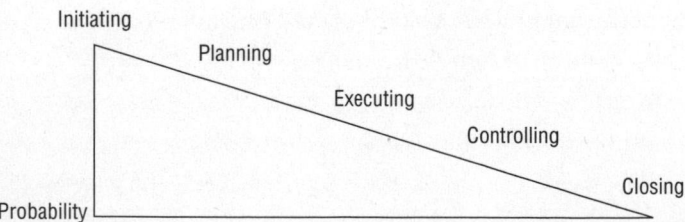

The opposite can be said for risk impact. At the beginning of the project, the impact of a risk event is less than it is later in the project life cycle—with the exception of the risk of your project being killed altogether.

Let's say the project is proceeding as planned for this example. Not a lot of energy or resource is usually expended in the Initiating phase of a project, so if a risk event occurs, the consequences it produces aren't likely devastating. For example, perhaps you're working on a software upgrade project. During the planning phase you discover that the software you're considering purchasing requires an upgrade of the operating system that lives on the servers and an upgrade of software on every desktop in your organization. Fortunately for you, you made this discovery during the planning phase. At this point, you can plan for an increase in the budget based on this new information, or the CIO can decide to kill the project and forgo installing the new software altogether with little organizational resource spent or lost.

The consequences or impact of this risk at this phase are minimal because the only resources usually expended at this point are human resources spent on planning, gathering information, and talking with stakeholders.

Now using the same example, imagine you've purchased the software and are in the later phases of the project. You've completed all the preliminary work and are ready to load the new software. Gulp. It isn't until now, somewhere in the Executing and Controlling phase, that you discover you also need to upgrade the server and desktops. The consequences of this occurring at this stage of the project are much higher. You've already put out the money for the software purchase, you've also spent company resources performing all the tasks of the project, and now you can't proceed without the operating system upgrade. The risk is much higher at this point in the project. The software you've purchased is useless without the other upgrades, and requesting additional funds at this point in the project may not fly (or be possible, depending on budget constraints). But, hey, the big boss can always use the paycheck of the project manager who allowed this risk event to occur to purchase the desktop and server upgrades once the project manager is gone.

The point is, the further you progress in the project life cycle, the less likely it is the risk event will occur, but the greater the impact to the project if the risk event does occur. The following graphic shows the inverse relationship of probability and impact as the project progresses through the life-cycle processes.

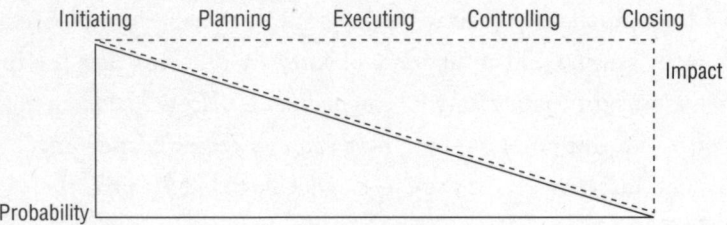

A Practical Risk Management Approach

In practical terms, a solid risk management methodology allows you to manage your project proactively. By that I mean you're in control and prepared for most anything that can happen on the project. On the other hand, reacting to events as they occur without any forethought regarding their probability of occurring (or what kind of trouble they could cause) is nothing more than crisis management.

A risk management approach starts first with the determination that you'll create and implement a risk management plan and not let problems run amok and get the upper hand. Identifying, analyzing, prioritizing, and then planning for the management of risks and monitoring the plans is a much better approach than allowing problems to change the outcome of your project because they weren't planned for ahead of time.

Earlier I talked about the five purposes for risk management. These are actually action items, or steps, you'll perform throughout the course of the project to actively engage in risk management. The Project Management

Institute's (PMI) *A Guide to the Project Management Body of Knowledge*—herein referred to as *A Guide to the PMBOK*—categorizes its Risk Management Knowledge Area into six processes. They are: Risk Management Planning, Risk Identification, Qualitative Risk Analysis, Quantitative Risk Analysis, Risk Response Planning, and Risk Monitoring and Control. Let's do a quick review of each of these processes next. As you've probably guessed, I'll be covering each of these areas more thoroughly as you progress through the book.

Risk Management Planning The purpose of the Risk Management Planning process is to create a *risk management plan*. Don't confuse this plan with the "what" of risk planning. The risk management plan is the "how" you'll go about dealing with risks on your project. It describes how you define, monitor, and control risks throughout the project. It also describes how each of the remaining processes in this knowledge area are implemented, monitored, and controlled throughout the life of the project. I'll discuss the risk management plan in more detail in the Risk Management Plan section later in this chapter.

Risk Identification The Risk Identification process involves identifying and documenting all the risks that could impact the project. This includes reviewing project documents, categorizing risks, reviewing checklists, using techniques such as brainstorming to identify risks, and ultimately producing a list of project risks. I'll discuss Risk Identification in detail in Chapter 2, "Identifying and Documenting Risks."

Qualitative Risk Analysis The purpose of the Qualitative Risk Analysis process is to determine the consequences the risks you identified in the Risk Identification process may have on the project objectives. It involves determining the probability that the risks will occur and ranking risks according to their effect on the project objectives. I'll discuss Qualitative Risk Analysis techniques in Chapter 5.

Quantitative Risk Analysis The Quantitative Risk Analysis process evaluates the impacts of risk and quantifies the overall risk exposure of the project by assigning numeric probabilities to each risk and their impacts on the project objectives. The primary output of this process is a prioritized list of quantified project risks. I'll cover Quantitative Risk Analysis techniques in Chapter 5.

Risk Response Planning Risk Response Planning involves deciding what actions to take to reduce threats while maximizing opportunities discovered during the performance of the risk processes. This process includes assigning staff members as risk owners. The risk owners are responsible for carrying out the risk response plans outlined during this process when the risk event occurs (or is about to occur). To read more about Risk Response Planning, see Chapter 6, "Defining Risk Response Plans."

Risk Monitoring and Control The purpose of the Risk Monitoring and Control process is to respond to risks as they occur, track and monitor identified risks, evaluate risk response plans for effectiveness, identify new risks, and ensure proper risk management procedures are being followed as defined in the risk management plan. I'll discuss Risk Monitoring and Control further in Chapter 7, "Implementing and Monitoring Risk Response Plans."

Table 1.1 ties *A Guide to the PMBOK*'s Risk Management Knowledge Area processes to the previous risk management action steps and the frequency or timing of each. Remember that while the risk management processes are broken out individually, many times you'll combine one or more of these processes into one step.

TABLE 1.1: Risk Management Processes and Purposes

PROCESS	ACTION STEP	TIMING
Risk Management Planning	Create risk management plan detailing how risks are managed for this project.	Once during Planning phase.
Risk Identification	Identify and document risks.	Ongoing throughout all phases of the project.
Qualitative Risk Analysis	Analyze and prioritize risks.	When new risks are identified.

TABLE 1.1 CONTINUED: Risk Management Processes and Purposes

PROCESS	ACTION STEP	TIMING
Quantitative Risk Analysis	Analyze and prioritize risks.	When new risks are identified.
Risk Response Planning	Create response plans and strategies for those risks with highest probability and impact.	When new risks are identified.
Risk Monitoring and Control	Monitor the effectiveness of the response plans.	Monitor response plans at project status meetings. Identify new risks and reevaluate throughout all project phases.
Risk Monitoring and Control	Perform risk audit and reviews to determine effectiveness of overall risk management plan.	Once during the Closing phase.

Now that I've covered the bases and we're all using the same risk process terminology, let's look closer at risks.

Risks versus Problems

Risks aren't problems. The problem is that the word *problems* is present tense. That is, they're in the process of occurring. Risks are potential events that threaten the work or completion of the project (or present the project team with opportunities). Therefore, a problem isn't a risk—it's a crisis.

Firefighters are trained to, well, put out fires. If you don't identify and plan for risks, you'll likely become a firefighter by default. While your fires aren't the life-threatening situations real firefighters put themselves into daily for our benefit (thank you!), they can burn you. Which of the following sounds more appealing to you?

- Arming yourself with the ability to anticipate when a risk event may occur and preparing plans that are ready to implement the minute you see smoke, thus preventing a major forest fire.

- Hosing down problems all around you as they spring up. And while you're doing that, stomping out the hot spots with your Harley-Davidson leather boots, never knowing for sure which one is the hottest and which one might sneak out of control and burn down the project while you're not looking.

Surely you chose the first bullet.

Unfortunately, we've all seen and experienced projects that are managed in crisis mode rather than proactive mode. It's a little like walking through the fun house at the amusement park and never knowing what's going to jump out at you next. All of us face those out-of-the-blue problems occasionally, but if this is the normal course of events on your projects, you should consider getting out of crisis management and into risk management. It's much safer work.

NOTE   Using proper risk management planning tools and techniques allows you to manage your project proactively instead of reactively.

Let's look at an example of risks versus problems. Remember, problems are events that are in the process of occurring with no forethought put into planning for their probability or impact.

Ned, a photojournalist friend I've just made up for purposes of this illustration, is on his way to his next assignment. He and three assistants are headed to Paris, France. Fortunately, one of Ned's assistants, Sherry, is trained in project management techniques and planned this assignment as a project (smart move). Ned, a brilliant photographer and writer, isn't a project manager—he deals with risks as they occur. Upon arriving in Paris, Ned and his co-workers are faced with one problem after the other. Table 1.2 shows a partial list of problems the group has encountered along with the reaction of Ned (the crisis manager) versus the proactive risk planning by the project manager.

TABLE 1.2: Firefighters versus Project Managers

CRISIS MANAGER (NED)	PROJECT MANAGER (SHERRY)
Lost passport	
Searches through every pocket of his carry-on bag while exclaiming, "I've lost my passport!"	Retrieves the photocopied page of the missing passport from the packet of travel documents collected before leaving on the assignment and presents it to an embassy representative for a passport replacement.
Missing luggage (the one with the camera equipment)	
After shouting expletives, asks the baggage claim attendant where the closest photography shop is located. The baggage claim attendant doesn't answer and pretends she can't speak English.	Has made arrangements with their regular photo supplier to send needed equipment overnight on a moment's notice. Also has previously separated the equipment into two or three bags so that not all the equipment is lost if a bag comes up missing.
Pouring rain the first day of the shoot	
Mopes and pouts about the bad weather while frantically searching for an alternative location to shoot so the whole day isn't lost.	Retrieves the project schedule and switches the indoor shoot (scheduled for day three) with today's activities.

As you can see, our project manager, Sherry, had a much better approach to each of these risks and was well prepared with plans in the event they occurred. Poor Ned was forced to deal with these situations as they came up. His reactions were a bit frazzled.

Risk Management Plan

You may be asking, "How do you go about implementing a practical approach to risk management without having to set up an entire department of folks to do it?" I'm glad you asked.

Your first order of business is creating a risk management plan. Remember that the risk management plan describes how you will go about defining and monitoring risks, not the specifics of how you'll deal with individual risks. (I'll get to the how-to specifics of performing the identification and planning processes in later chapters.)

NOTE The risk management plan describes how each of the risk processes (Risk Identification, Qualitative Risk Analysis, Quantitative Risk Analysis, Risk Response Planning, and Risk Monitoring and Control) will be implemented, monitored, and controlled throughout the life of the project.

The primary elements of a risk management plan are as follows:

Methodology This section describes what methods you'll use to perform risk management. For example, you'd describe the types of techniques you'll use to identify risks, how you'll document your risk information, and perhaps how you'll tackle determining risk response plan strategies. It should also describe how newly identified risks are reported to the project manager.

Roles and responsibilities This section includes the roles of all the major stakeholders (including you as the project manager) as it pertains to risk identification and control and, most important, the roles of the risk owners, including their responsibilities in implementing and monitoring response plans.

Budget Medium-to-large-sized projects, or those with an extraordinary amount of risks with high impacts, may have a special budget for managing risk. If a risk budget exists, it's documented here.

Risk scoring Qualitative and quantitative analysis processes are used to rank and score risks. You can use several methods to do this, which you'll explore in Chapter 5. This section of the risk management plan should include a description of the scoring method you'll use, how you developed the scoring method, and the thresholds that indicate you should develop and implement a response plan.

Reporting formats This section should detail how the risk management information will be maintained, updated, and reported to project participants.

Tracking This section includes a description of the how you'll document the history of the risk activities for the current project and how the risk processes will be audited. You can refer to this information as you progress through the project and also when you work on future projects that are similar to this one.

NOTE   You can find a copy of a Risk Management Plan template for your use on the Sybex website at www.sybex.com.

Risk Triggers

Imagine this: You and a group of friends (along with half the population of the city) stake out a spot to watch the annual fireworks show. You spread out a blanket, pull out the pop and snacks from your backpack, and create a nice spread. A thunderous boom sounds in the distance. Everyone looks up, anticipating the first brilliant display. What they see instead is a streak of lightning followed by another boom—a sure sign everyone ought to pack up and head for safety.

Risk triggers are signs that a risk event is about to occur. Like the thunder example, a risk trigger signals that something bigger is on the horizon. Watching for risk triggers is an important activity in your overall risk management approach. You and your team members should always be on the lookout for risk triggers. Like the thunder example, they'll signal you that a risk event is approaching.

Watch for risk triggers from the team members themselves as well. For example, a team member who previously seemed happy and upbeat about the project begins joking about finding another job or making comments that you can get along just fine without them. These statements, obviously, could signal that the team member really is thinking of leaving. The bad news concerning this risk trigger is that schedule delays or increased costs may result. Heed what your team members are saying and evaluate it in light of project risks, even when they act like they're joking.

Continuous Process

Risk management isn't a one-person job—unless your project is extremely small and you aren't only the project manager but the project team as well. Even then, you still have a project sponsor, a boss who you report to, and stakeholders who will benefit from the project's completion. Each of these folks can help you remain on the lookout for risk triggers, identify and prioritize risks, and identify response plans to deal with the risks.

Risk management is a continuous, iterative process oftentimes called *progressive elaboration*. New risks can appear at any point in the project. They're more likely to occur early on in the project's life cycle, but don't let that lull you into a false sense of security. Remain on the lookout for new risks and for risk triggers throughout all the phases of the project. Continuously monitor response plans that have been implemented, and, last but not least, don't be a firefighter—be a risk manager!

Communication Is the Key

I can't say it enough—communicating is the most important responsibility you have as a project manager. Ninety percent of your time is spent in this activity. I can't think of any other element that has a greater impact on your project's success than good communication. And like risk management, good project communications starts with a plan.

The Communications Plan

The communications planning process says that all projects should have a communications management plan. I refer to this plan as the Big Picture plan because it tells me at a glance who the key stakeholders are, what their information needs are, how they want the information reported, when they want the information distributed, and the format of the delivery. I can tell from this plan who should be the first one notified when a risk event takes a turn for the worse and who to call when it's time to celebrate a success. I require a communications plan (along with a scope statement, risk plan, and project schedule) for all projects our department undertakes, no matter how small or large the project is.

The communications plan works together with the risk management plan to determine who, how, and when information regarding the status of risks and the progress of the response plans gets reported.

NOTE The risk plan details how you'll carry out the risk processes, and the communications plan documents how the information regarding the status of the processes gets communicated and to what parties.

Communicating risk status is just as important to the health of the project as communicating overall project status. It's a good idea to devote a portion of every project status meeting to risk status. This is an opportunity to review the key risks that you have identified and check the pulse of those risk events that still appear dormant. You should also review any response plans in place as a result of a risk event and discuss the effectiveness of the risk plan. This is also an opportunity to identify new risks and watch for risk triggers.

Exchanging Information

Communicating is the process of exchanging information. Communication has three parts: a sender, the message, and a receiver. You and I are actively engaged in communicating now. I'm the sender. I've used the written form of communication to prepare this book that you're reading. If I were speaking about this information at a conference where you were an audience participant, all the components of the information exchange still exist, but the form of the communication changes to verbal.

As the project manager, you'll use plenty of both forms of communication. You'll also act as both sender and receiver of information. For example, your risk management plan, risk response plans, risk lists, and so on should all take the written form. When you're providing risk status to stakeholders or instructing team members on the course of action to take when a risk event occurs, you may use both written and verbal forms.

It's a Two-Way Street

Information exchange is a two-way street. Both the sender and the receiver have responsibilities to assure the message is clear and understood as it was intended.

Senders make certain the information is clear and precise and is presented to the receivers in a way that is easily understood by the receivers. For example, if I were speaking to a group of high schoolers on the topic of risk management, my approach and the content of my message would be much different than if I were speaking with project management professionals with years of hands-on experience under their belts.

Receivers, likewise, share in the responsibility of communicating clearly. Receivers have a tendency to filter the information they hear through their own perceptions. For example, if I told you that risk management planning should only be performed on large projects, you'd probably start tuning me out because you know that information isn't correct.

Table 1.3 shows the relationship between senders and receivers and the responsibility each has in the communication exchange.

TABLE 1.3: Senders and Receivers in the Information Exchange

SENDERS' RESPONSIBILITY	RECEIVERS' RESPONSIBILITY
Make the message clear and concise.	Read and listen to the message for understanding.
Target the information for the right audience.	Avoid jumping to conclusions. Interpret the information at face value.
Avoid unnecessary detail and technical jargon.	Ask clarifying questions.
Keep it honest.	Control your emotions.

Active Listening

I believe one of the most important duties you have as a receiver is to practice active listening. You may think this applies only to situations where someone is speaking to you, but you can practice active listening when reading as well. I've listed some pointers for active listening techniques in both the written and verbal forms of communication.

The following are active listening techniques for written forms of communication:

- Scan the document first for key issues.

- Paraphrase what you read in your own words.

- Read the document for understanding without filtering it through your emotions or perceptions.

- Recognize cultural differences in the presentation of the information.

The following are active listening techniques for verbal forms of communication:

- Show genuine interest in the speaker by nodding in agreement and asking questions when appropriate.

- Make eye contact with the speaker.

- Focus on the topic at hand.

- Refrain from interrupting.

- Ask clarifying questions.

- Paraphrase what you heard.

Communication is a critical component of successful risk management. While you can't know it all, even with good communication, establishing effective working relationships and open lines of communication with your project team members and stakeholders will keep the information exchange flowing. Half the battle is getting the information in the first place; the other half is what you do with it once you have it. Likewise, the amount and method of communication also has an impact on the risk impact and consequences.

Unspoken Clues

If you knew everything there was to know about the project, there would be no risk and, hence, no reason for this book.

Back to reality—this scenario doesn't exist. It isn't possible for you to know everything. Thankfully, you do know certain things about your project and you can use certain techniques for increasing the amount of information you have. More information means an increased ability to determine risk and the predictability of the risks outcomes and impacts. One of the most important ways to increase the amount of information you have is through communication. Get out there and talk to your team members and stakeholders. Get a feel for their attitudes about how the project is progressing and whether they feel risk events are imminent. But keep an eye out for the unspoken attitudes and shifts in attention or mood. This is where you may very well realize a risk event is about to occur, or a new risk identified, that you wouldn't have found any other way.

Let's look at some of the other more subtle dynamics you should watch for when interacting with project participants.

Clues from stakeholders Especially listen for things they don't necessarily intend to tell you. For example, while discussing one of the risk events with a stakeholder, she tells you, "Don't worry about Jerry; he won't be a problem." Every project you've ever worked on that required help from Jerry or his group took every ounce of negotiation and finagling you could drum up to get him to cooperate. This statement may be hinting that Jerry is moving on to another company. However, until you know the facts, continue planning as though you'll have to work with him.

Bad attitudes and lack of motivation These are always signs that trouble is brewing with the team. Spend some one-on-one time with key team members to determine the cause. Perhaps they're not in agreement with a recent project decision or the direction things are headed. Don't ignore their insights. Simply taking the time to hear them out may be all that's needed to get them back on track.

Body language This is another silent clue that something more is going on than what's being said. Again, don't hesitate to ask questions and give folks an opportunity to tell you what they're thinking.

Lack of participation Key team members hem and haw when they're usually forthright with their opinions. They don't participate in discussions or put forth lackluster ideas. A long list of issues could be going on here—everything from personal issues to project issues. If it's project issues, you want to know about them. If it's personal issues and this employee is a key project member, you need to know enough of the situation to assess the risks and plan accordingly.

High absenteeism The same thing applies here as the previous bullet. The reasons could be wholly uninvolved with the project, but then again, trouble could be brewing. Do yourself and the project a favor and check into it.

Stay attuned to what you're hearing and what your gut reactions are telling you and follow up on them. It's important to gather as much information as you can, and paying attention to the factors listed previously are a good place to start. I encourage you to not jump to conclusions in any of these situations. Ask questions and get the facts so you'll have concrete information to determine if threats and opportunities exist. As the project manager, your primary responsibility is to satisfactorily complete the goals of the project on time, on budget, within scope, and while meeting or exceeding stakeholder expectations. The remainder of this book will discuss the approaches and techniques you can use to identify, analyze, and plan for risks. In turn, this helps you keep your executives, stakeholders, and project team members informed and your project headed toward a successful completion.

Case Study

Emily Lewis is a well-respected team leader with Customer Centric Company. Customer Centric is an upstart company that markets credit-card-processing services to businesses. This includes the card-swipe machines that you see at every check stand and, most important, the processing of the credit transactions.

Emily was recently named the project manager for a new project the CIO has dubbed CIP (he pronounces it "sip"), which stands for Customer Information Integration Project.

Customer Centric currently has a homegrown customer relationship management software program. Their current program performs the following functions:

- Maintains customer account information

- Tracks customer queries

- Contains a basic knowledge tree with answers to common questions

Customer Centric has two call centers staffed with 30 to 50 people each. Each call center serves two functions: it addresses customer questions about their service, and it is a telemarketing center that makes and sets up appointments for salespeople in the field.

The current customer relationship management program (CRM) system doesn't interface with the company's enterprise resource planning (ERP) system. That means call center folks must access two separate systems when talking with customers. They must go to the CRM system to get the customer account information and to track the customer query and then log onto the ERP system to obtain accounting and inventory information. The ERP system performs the following functions:

- Tracks accounts receivable

- Tracks accounts payable

- Maintains manufacturing information such as inventory counts of card-swipe machines and inventory of parts

- Maintains human resource data including payroll, benefits tracking, job applications, and performance reviews

The objective of the CIP project is to purchase a new CRM package that integrates with the existing ERP system and thereby increases the efficiency of the call center, decreases average call times, and increases customer satisfaction levels of call center calls. The new system will also allow the tracking of sales calls and the recording of the result of the sales appointment.

The sales staff in the field can be notified of new appointments via e-mail, fax, or text messaging to their mobile phones. The sales staff will access the CRM system via the Internet to record the results of their sales calls.

Emily is fairly new to the project management field. She has had great success with a handful of small projects but has never worked on any project this large. This is considered a medium-sized project from the organization's perspective. From Emily's perspective, she views it as huge. She wants to assure this project is a success. She has already signed up to attend some project management training classes, but she won't get everything she needs fast enough to kick this project off; therefore, she bought some books in the Spotlight Series to help her.

Emily has documented the goals of the project, and the scope statement was agreed to and signed by the executive sponsor (her CIO, Bill Olsen) and the key stakeholders (whom you'll meet in later chapters). She has reviewed the risk processes with her project team, and her next task includes preparing the risk management plan. In the risk management plan, she'll document the following:

Methodology

The processes for identifying and documenting risks (I'll talk about these in Chapter 2)

The processes for analyzing and prioritizing risks

The methods for developing risk response plans

The methods for monitoring risk response plans

Roles and responsibilities

The roles and responsibilities of risk reporters

The roles and responsibilities of risk owners

The roles and responsibilities of the project sponsor, project manager, and project team members in risk management

Budget

The budget amount for risk response plans

The budget amount for contingencies

Reporting and tracking formats

The recording mechanism for risks and response plans

The tracking mechanism for updating risk lists and response plans

The reporting formats for updating the project stakeholders regarding risks

I'll discuss each of these sections and the ideas presented at length in the chapters to come. Remember that Emily has already read the entire book, so she knows what information to plug into each of these sections.

CHAPTER 2

Identifying and Documenting Risks

In this chapter, I'll discuss the how-tos of managing risks. The first step, of course, is to identify risks. I'll start by discussing a high-level overview of the identification process. This will include looking at categories of risks and describing the types of risks you may encounter on a typical project.

Then I'll show you places to look to uncover risks, who to ask for assistance in the process, and some techniques for generating ideas.

Next I'll discuss the importance of documenting risks. This will include a description of the difference between risk originators and risk owners. Finally, I'll wrap up with a checklist of the steps involved in the risk identification process that you can use on your next project.

Identifying Risks

Since project managers (PMs) primarily focus on the negative aspects of risk—okay, the really bad things that can happen and ultimately prevent us from completing the project—identifying risks is a little like playing the pessimist. The sky could fall in, a key team member could win the mega-jackpot, or the big boss could decide to switch gears on everyone and cancel the project altogether. But the purpose of this process isn't to play the pessimist. The purpose is to identify risks so that you can analyze them for their impact on the project and determine which ones need response plans. Additionally, risk identification involves identifying *risk triggers*, which are signs or symptoms that tell you a risk event is about to occur.

It's important to have a plan that describes how you'll go about managing risks, as I discussed in the last chapter. Identifying risks is the first action step you'll perform in your overall risk management strategy. This step starts you on the way to effectively dealing with tangible risks that may affect your project.

Identifying risks requires some prep work. So first, gather a few of your project planning documents including the following:

- Scope statement
- Resource requirements
- Work breakdown structure
- Risk management plan
- Cost estimates
- Project schedule
- Historical information

The first place to start is with historical information. Historical information includes documentation, lessons learned, and project information from other projects similar in scope or size to the project on which you're working.

NOTE   It's always a good idea to review historical information from past projects before beginning risk planning on a new project. Make certain you're examining past projects that are similar in size and complexity to your current project.

There's great value in learning from your predecessors and even greater value in not repeating their mistakes. Historical information will tell you the types of risks previous PMs experienced on similar projects, the responses they developed for the risks, and how effective those responses were. This is the first place I always begin when starting a new project and when identifying risks.

Categories

Several elements will help make your risk identification process go smoothly. The first is determining risk categories.

Risk categories provide a way for you to organize the risks of your project into logical groupings. Ultimately, at the end of this process you want to end up with a list of risks, their descriptions, their impacts, their categories, and so on that you'll track in a database or spreadsheet program. You can download a Risk List template from www.sybex.com to help get you started with this process. According to *A Guide to the PMBOK*, at least four categories of risk exist, as follows:

- Technical, quality, and performance
- Project management
- Organizational
- External

Table 2.1 describes each of these categories. I believe many more categories can and should be defined for your project. Limiting yourself to four doesn't provide you the breadth needed to cover all the potential risk events for every project.

Your organization, typically, should define the risk categories so they reflect those risks applicable to their business and industry. But if your experience is like mine, you'll have to start from scratch and develop them yourself. I'll help you do that by listing the categories and describing each. Feel free to modify these categories and descriptions to best fit your organization and the project. Keep in mind that not all categories will apply to all projects or industries. That reminds me: some industries may have category lists already predefined. Check your local chapters or well-respected industry websites and use them in conjunction with those shown in Table 2.1. If your organization has a Project Management Office (PMO), check with them as well.

TABLE 2.1: Risk Categories

CATEGORY	DESCRIPTION
Internal	Risks that come from within the project or organization.
External	Risks that come from outside the project or organization.
Financial	Risks associated with revenues, profits, return on investment calculations, project budgets, project costs, and the like.
Technical and performance	Risks associated with the technical aspects of the project. This could be information technology–related (as in hardware or software) or industry specific such as engineering diagrams, mechanical equipment, building support systems (such as HVAC and fire suppression), and so on. Performance risks may involve unproven or complex technology or may involve unrealistic performance goals or measures.
Business	Risks associated with marketing or timing of product releases, vendor delays, management issues, competitor information, and so on.
Organizational	Risks associated with the organization itself.
Cultural	Risks associated with cultural issues or differences (this especially applies to organizations that have an international presence).
Security	Risks associated with information security, security of personnel, security of assets, and security of intellectual property.
Project management	Risks associated with project management processes, organizational maturity, and ability.
Legal	Risks associated with legal issues that may impact the project or the organization.
Environmental	Risks associated with the project that may have environmental impacts.
Scope	Risks that impact the scope of the project.
Quality	Risks that impact the quality of the project or the product of the project.
Schedule	Risks associated with activity estimating and schedules.
Process	Risks associated with the business processes or other processes that impact the organization, the customer, or the project.

Don't stop with just this list. Use some of the techniques I'll talk about in the "How to Look for Risk" section later in this chapter to engage your team members and stakeholders in defining the categories that apply to your project and organization. You can even define these categories into subcategories.

Table 2.2 shows an example of the subcategories possible for the business and technical categories defined in Table 2.1.

TABLE 2.2: Risk Subcategories

BUSINESS RISK SUBCATEGORIES	TECHNICAL RISK SUBCATEGORIES
Marketing	Hardware
Management issues	Software
Cyclical risks	Database
Vendor issues	Integration
Timing	Scalability

Obviously, you could create subcategories for all the categories listed in Table 2.1. Depending on the complexity of the project and the propensity for risk events (that is, are there a lot of risk events associated with your project or only a few?), you may consider creating subcategories after your categories are established.

Risk categories will come in handy later in the risk management process to help establish priorities. For example, your project may not have any legal risks, but technical and environmental risks are both possible. If you know ahead of time that your organization will not tolerate environmental risk, you'll be able to more easily assign risk priorities.

Risk Types

You could further categorize risks into risk types. By this I mean financial risks, human resource risks, technology risks, and so on. In my opinion, defining categories and types of risks for small-to-medium-sized projects can be overkill. I think you'll find categories are sufficient to describe your risks. When you get into larger projects, further classification of risks into risk types can be beneficial because it provides an efficient way to store and sort data.

Once you've established your risk categories, you should consider getting a feel for the level of heartburn these categories cause your senior management team or client. I'll talk more about this in the "Risk Tolerance" section of Chapter 5, "Analyzing and Prioritizing Risks."

Once you've determined the risk categories, you don't have a big need to do this again. You should repeat the remaining steps, however, periodically throughout the project. You can use the risk categories and risk types to help identify risks later in the project as it progresses. I make it a habit to spend time at every project status meeting discussing risks and examining our assumptions, the existing risk list, and any new events that occurred that may trigger a risk. Reviewing the risk categories provides the team with a quick way to fully extend their risk antenna and think about recent events they may lead to a risk.

Common Risks

Now that you have an understanding of the risk categories, let's examine the risks themselves. The purpose here is to begin the processes of identifying risks that may affect your project. You shouldn't be worried—yet—about their specific impact to the project. I'll talk about that in Chapter 5.

The following lists common and not-so-common risks. Please realize this list isn't exhaustive and is in no particular order. It's intended to give you a place to start, but it's not intended to replace your own information-gathering and identification techniques. I'll talk about the specific techniques of identifying risks on your project in the "How to Look for Risks" section later in this chapter.

Loss of key employee	Inadequate project budgets	Cost overruns
Funding cuts	Stakeholder consensus	Environmental threats

Weather	Unrealistic quality objectives	Labor strikes or work stoppages
Complex technology	New, unproven technology	Availability of resources and materials
Unrealistic performance goals	Immeasurable performance standards	Changes in key stakeholders
Lack of involvement by project sponsor	Loss of project sponsor during course of the project	Changes in the company's ownership
Resistance to change (as a result of the implementation of the project)	Seasonal and cyclical events (for example, hurricanes, tourist season, and holiday sales)	Availability of business expert
Availability of technical experts	Knowledge and skills of business and technical experts	Organizational structure (to whom do team members report?)
Cultural barriers (diversity, corporate culture, and international projects)	Theft of customer data or company information	Skills and ability of project team members given the size and complexity of the project and their past experience
Skills and ability of the project manager given the size and complexity of the project and their past experience	Skills and ability of the business users and subject matter experts given the size and complexity of the project and their past experience	Vendor ability and skills given the size and complexity of the project and their past experience

Vendor and suppliers availability	Financial stability of vendor and suppliers	Unrealistic or incomplete scope definition
Scope statement not agreed to by all stakeholders	Unrealistic or incomplete schedule development	Inaccurate estimates

---

NOTE Scope and schedule risks are two of the biggest risks you'll encounter on most projects. I've devoted Chapter 4, "Preventing Scope and Schedule Risks," to this topic.

Catastrophic Risks

Ned, our photojournalist friend from Chapter 1, learned a new term while he was in Paris. The term is *force majeure* (this term is used in the United States also). Force majeure describes risks that are so catastrophic that they're outside the scope of risk management planning. The following are some examples of force majeure risks that I hope you never have to deal with:

Forces of nature Earthquakes, hurricanes, floods, volcanoes, meteorites, and unpredictable weather

External forces Government action, civil unrest, acts of war, terrorist acts, and social instability

External forces are of particular concern when working on projects in third-world countries and countries with unstable governments or civil unrest. I recommend you spend time researching any country you plan on working in to assess the potential for these events.

Risks Lurking in the Processes

As I discussed in Chapter 1, "What Is Risk Management," risks are more likely to occur early in the project and decrease in probability as the project progress. When you're in the process of identifying risks, think about the life-cycle process of the project. Especially concentrate on the Initiating, Planning, and Executing phases, as this is where the greatest opportunity exists for risks to occur. For example, during Initiating, anything can happen. The project justification itself may prove the project is too risky to undertake.

Have I mentioned that risk identification is an ongoing process? Don't forget to review your risk lists as you progress through the project. I recommend reviewing your risk list at the beginning of each life-cycle phase, at a minimum.

NOTE The Executing phase of the project is particularly vulnerable to risk. The work of the project happens during this phase, which means the probability for risks occurring is high. And the risk impacts hit harder during this phase than earlier phases. Since some of the work of the project is either started or completed by this stage, significant resources and time have been invested. This is often the phase where projects that are in trouble are kept alive because of all the resources expended to date.

Table 2.3 shows a partial list of the some of the more common project risks. I've placed an X in the column indicating the phase this risk is likely to occur in or the phase with the greatest impact. It doesn't mean this is the only phase where this risk can occur, so stay tuned in throughout the project. This is a guideline to give you an idea of what to look for during the different life-cycle phases of the project.

TABLE 2.3: Occurrence of Risks in the Life Cycle

RISK	INIT	PLAN	EXEC	CONT	CLOSE
Project schedule		X	X	X	
Stakeholder consensus	X	X			
Scope changes		X	X		
Inaccurate estimates	X	X			
Loss of key employee		X	X	X	X

You may be asking, why is the loss of a key employee a big risk in the closing phase? The reason is the employee could walk away with project knowledge or expertise that could be used on a future project. I talked about historical information earlier in this chapter. A large portion of historical information comes from project team members. So make certain you conduct an exit interview with team members who leave the project before it's completed. Document their knowledge of the project, the elements of the project they think worked well and those that didn't work well, and how those processes could be improved on future projects. Speaking of team members, let's look at one more project risk before moving on to "Where to Look."

People Risk

People are people. And one thing is certain—you can't complete the work of the project without them. If you've been a project manager for long, you probably also know that along with scope and schedule risks, people are one of the biggest problems...I mean, risks...you'll encounter on any project.

In the not-too-distant past, jobs in this country were primarily blue-collar or labor intensive in nature. Folks had factory jobs or worked the farm, for example. They were employed for the work they could perform with their hands. Their workday was very structured and their tasks completely defined for them. For example, "Weld Panel A to Panel B in these precise spots using silver solder," and so on.

Today, in the age of information, many of our jobs require the use of our knowledge or the use of our knowledge in combination with the work of our hands. The medical field, for example, requires extensive knowledge coupled with hands-on skill at performing tasks. Information technology, engineering, and research require specialized training and knowledge. Often it takes folks with these types of skills to perform the work of the project. The problem is the productivity of these folks is largely determined from within themselves. In factory-based work, for example, we know employees can fasten a specified number of widgets to a part in one hour.

If employees consistently miss this mark, we take action to help them meet the performance goal or replace the employee. It's difficult (if not impossible in some instances) to define productivity goals for knowledge-based workers as they determine how much or how little they'll produce in a given day. I had a programmer on my team once...well, I won't go there.

Don't underestimate the importance of the people factor on your project. We don't usually take the time to think about the types of risks associated with individuals on the project. Yes, we do think about key folks leaving and the impact that will have on the project. But what about other factors?

- Lack of motivation resulting in low productivity or missed deadlines

- Dishonesty resulting in inaccurate reports or inaccurate estimates

- Theft of real and intellectual property resulting in financial loss and legal issues

- Low productivity resulting in missed deadlines and higher costs

- Sabotage resulting in poor quality, missed deadlines, and strife with other team members

- Absenteeism resulting in missed deadlines and higher project costs

- Lack of documentation resulting in missed opportunities on future projects

- Lawsuits, harassment claims, and workers' comp, resulting in missed deadlines and increased costs

If your project team members are new or you've never worked with them before, take the time to interview them before assigning them to project tasks. You could also have trusted team members assist you with this. It's better to know in the interview stage if team members have a potential for the risks listed previously than in the midst of the project.

Where to Look

Now you know what you're looking for, so the next question is, where do you look? It's time to put on your detective's decoder ring.

Like all good detectives, PMs need to start with a few questions. You know—establish the basics, and find out who is telling the truth. The one question you should always be thinking about when looking for risk is what would happen if...? and then fill in the blank. For example, what would happen if electricity wasn't available during implementation? What would happen if the supplier couldn't deliver materials as promised? What would happen if the engineer miscalculated load capacity?

TIP   Most great novelists start new book projects by asking the what would happen if... question. They don't stop there. They keep asking the question throughout the novel and come up with wonderful twists and turns they wouldn't have thought of earlier in the process. It's a great technique for you to use on your project as well. What would happen if...you applied this technique on your next project?

The following is another list of questions to ask. You'll identify many project risks simply by examining the answers to these. Get out your magnifying glass here, though. You aren't looking for the obvious answers. You're looking for the what would happen if...? at the core of these questions. If the goal of your project is to move company headquarters from one location to another, what would happen if the existing tenants don't move out as promised or (heaven forbid) one of the moving trucks full of company files overturns on the highway? Think at this level when answering these questions.

- What is the goal of the project?
- What are the project deliverables?
- What are the critical success factors?
- How many resources do we have?

- What are the skill levels of each resource?
- How much time do we have to complete the project?
- Who are the project's stakeholders?

From here, you'll start examining your project documents. I've already talked about historical information. This is a great place to start. Past projects that are similar in size, complexity, and scope to the current project are worth investigating. Look at the risk list developed for those projects, but concentrate most of your time examining the response plans and their results. This will indicate the types of risks that may occur on the current project and their possible impacts.

Next, grab the project planning documents and start reviewing them while wearing your detective's decoder ring. Keep asking what would happen if...? The following are some of the project planning documents and elements you should examine when identifying risks:

- Scope statement
- Critical success factors
- Activity list
- Quality plan
- Project schedule
- Project budget
- Resource assignments
- Organizational structure
- Procurement procedures
- Work breakdown structure

In addition to reviewing your project plans, you can also use a risk checklist as a source of potential project risks. Checklists may exist in your organization from past projects, or one may have been developed for the purposes of risk management. You may work in a certain industry, like engineering, for example, that has its own industry standards and checklists, so check with a local industry chapter or browse their Internet sites. Use these checklists when identifying your risks, as some of the hard work may already be done for you. It will also give you some insight into the kinds of risks your organization considers most likely to occur.

NOTE You can also use the list from the earlier "Common Risks" as a checklist. You'll find a copy of this checklist at www.sybex.com: it's titled Checklist of Common Risks.

Work Breakdown Structure

Another project planning document you'll find useful in your hunt for risks is the work breakdown structure *(WBS)*. The WBS displays the work of the project in hierarchical fashion. The first level of the WBS depicts the project, the next level the project deliverables, and so on from there. Depending on the level of detail contained on the WBS, it may show activities as well.

The following illustration shows a partial WBS for Ned's photo-shoot project. Sherry, the project manager for this endeavor, constructed it. (We all know by now that Ned wouldn't do something like this!)

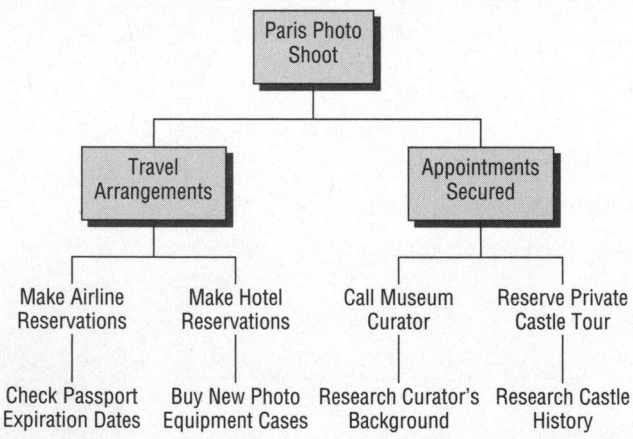

You can see that Sherry must have used the what would happen if...? question when examining the WBS. The activity titled "Check passport expiration dates" could have generated a question about what would happen if Ned lost his passport. The answer generated a potential risk. And it helped the project manager develop a strategy for dealing with the risk. The same thing happened for the activity titled "Buy new photo equipment cases."

Use your project's WBS in a similar fashion. Don't just take it at face value. Think of all the situations in which Ned could find himself!

Assumptions and Constraints

Assumptions are events or actions believed to be true. As you know, these should be documented. The reason I bring them up now is because part of your risk management approach should include assumptions analysis. By that I mean you should periodically review the assumptions made about the project and analyze them to determine if they're still valid.

NOTE   Assumptions analysis is a tool and technique of the risk identification process.

For example, maybe way back in the Initiation process one project assumption was stated as "Jessica Morgan will fill the lead programmer role for the duration of the project." Everyone assumed and believed Jessica would be available to head the programming team. Now, midway through the project, you reexamine that assumption and realize that Jessica is getting a promotion next month. This assumption is no longer valid; in fact, you have identified a project risk.

Constraints are another place to look for project risk. Constraints either limit or dictate the actions of the project team. Constraints typically concern issues dealing with project scope, time, quality issues, or project costs.

The following illustration depicts a project with equally balanced constraints.

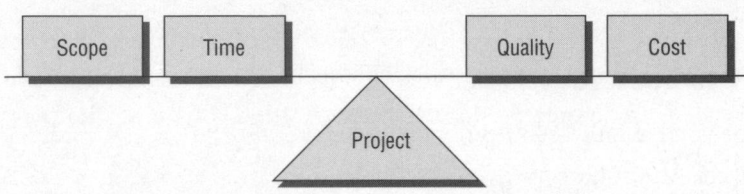

That's a great picture of a perfect world, however; most projects don't have equally balanced constraints. The problem (and the opportunity for those of you looking for risks) is when one or two constraints are out of proportion to the others. For example, your project sponsor informed you that the project deadline must be shortened. That means you can no longer keep the constraints in balance. If time is shortened, something else must give. You can't continue to have the same level of quality, complete the same number of deliverables, keep the costs the same, *and* shorten the time. So you'll have to trim some elements from the project's scope to meet the new time constraint. The costs are going up because now you'll need contractors to help you finish by the new deadline. Scope and time have decreased, costs have increased, and quality remains the same. The following illustration shows an example of the new project constraints and their proportions.

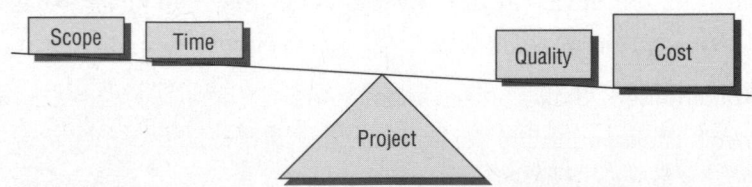

So when you're looking for places that may harbor risks, examine the constraint list. Most certainly put that detective's decoder ring back on anytime the constraints change. In the previous example, the project end date was shortened. New risks that could occur as a result of this change include lack of available resources, poor quality because the project team "gets it done" without regard to specifications, cost overruns (even with a revised project budget), and poor quality.

How to Look for Risk

I hope you haven't been thinking you need to do all this identification by yourself. Although your own experience with project management techniques and your exposure to projects of similar size and scope to your current project will prove invaluable, you need to include the expertise of others as well. It isn't likely that you or anyone else could think of every potential project risk. Each team member and stakeholder brings a unique view to the project, and their perspective on what can happen is exactly what you want to tap.

Who to Ask

So, you ask, who do you ask? I'm glad you asked. The following are most of the key folks you should consider including in your risk identification activity and the value they bring to this process:

Project sponsor Other participants may not have the strategic vision the sponsor has, so this person is in a unique position to identify risks others may not know.

Project team members Make certain to tap team member's knowledge once the work has commenced.

Stakeholders Stakeholders understand the risks associated with their own business units and the business aspects of the project, which gives them a unique perspective.

Technical experts These folks have specific knowledge related to the technical aspects of the project. Information technology experts, engineers, researchers, construction specialists, policy makers, and business process experts are a few examples.

Customers and end users The customer, or end user, understands the goals of the project from a different perspective than the other project participants.

Vendors Vendors likely have experience working on projects of a similar nature and have insight to risks that may occur in all stages of the project.

Other project managers Don't hesitate to ask other project managers in other units for their thoughts regarding your project's risks. They're also a good source for reviewing the final risk list you'll compile at the end of this process.

People with previous experience Don't forget about the employee who has extensive experience in one area of the business but has just transferred to a new work unit.

Industry groups You can tap other organizations, such as the Project Management Institute (PMI) or the Institute of Electrical and Electronics Engineers (IEEE).

TIP Having other team members assist you with the risk management action steps (such as identification, prioritization, and response planning) helps reduce overall project risk. Involving others gives you a broader perspective of the answers to the what if...? question and helps ensure your response plans are thorough and effective.

Before you invite these folks to the identification party, start by reviewing your risk categories. Categories help you identify who to ask, because if you know, for example, that financial risks are likely on this project, you'll want to include someone from the accounting or finance group to help with the process.

Gathering Information

Probably the biggest how-to of the risk identification process concerns gathering the information. The purpose is to derive accurate, reliable information regarding project risks that you can further analyze and prioritize.

You should know a few pointers before you get into the how-to techniques themselves. First, don't spend too much time on this process. The goal here is to identify the risks—not discuss them, define plans, or figure out their impacts. Act quickly, and get the risks written down in list form. The best ideas usually occur early in the meetings but not always. One idea leads to another and another, which is one of the benefits of involving more than one person in the risk identification process.

Have a plan for any of the techniques you plan on using—don't wing it. It's frustrating for a stakeholder—or anyone for that matter—to think their time is being wasted. Develop an action plan before meeting with folks or calling them together so you can finish the process quickly and remain productive as possible during the meeting. Understand the differences in these techniques and when to use them.

TIP   Many of the risks you'll uncover concern scope, time, quality, and cost issues. Funny thing is—they sound a lot like constraints. Since constraints limit or dictate project team actions, it makes sense that risks may be lurking in these areas. Pose questions and guide the risk identification team to examine these four constraints when developing your risk list.

The information-gathering techniques I'll talk about next are great techniques to put to use right away for identifying risks. Keep in mind that these techniques are useful for any process where information is needed from several people such as gathering requirements, defining assumptions, identifying quality measures, and so on. I recommend you limit the number of participants in group meetings. Once you approach more than nine or ten members, the communication exchange becomes unwieldy and it's difficult for the facilitator to keep the group on track.

Interviews

The interviewing technique involves question-and-answer sessions with experts, stakeholders, managers, project team members, or others who can assist you with identifying risks. You'll want to interview those who have knowledge of the project, the business processes, or the customer, for example. Don't forget other project managers or those who have experience on similar projects as sources. Sometimes folks who don't have specific knowledge of your project may also prove a great source of risk knowledge.

Be prepared with questions and some documentation before starting the interview. Since you're on a risk hunt (sounds like something from a horror movie, doesn't it?), be certain to ask the open-ended question, what would happen if...? to your interviewees. If you're interviewing an end user, for example, ask them what would happen if the product wasn't completed by the due date. Or, what would happen if the product was completed by the due date but was missing key features?

Take along the scope document and your WBS to give the folks you're interviewing an overview of the project and the key deliverables. This should help get their imaginations rolling.

TIP After you've asked your questions, make certain to give the folks you're interviewing time to tell you what their perceptions of the project are and if they know of any questions you should ask other stakeholders.

Interviewing is a technique you can apply to any project. Small, medium, and large projects will benefit from the expert opinions of others.

Brainstorming

Brainstorming is a facilitated exchange of information. A group of stakeholders, project team members, and others are asked to meet and identify possible risk events. This process requires a facilitator (that's usually you) who records the risks one by one on a whiteboard where all participants can see them. I also recommend you have someone else besides yourself recording the risks and ideas on a notepad or laptop. Ideally, you'd ask one of the participants or a fellow team member to help you with this task prior to the meeting. This way, the pressure to facilitate and record everything is shared instead of resting solely on your shoulders.

You don't need too much preparation for this technique. Check the room before the meeting, and make certain it is equipped with a whiteboard or a flip chart and fresh markers. Ask each of the participants to think about project risks before arriving. Coach them to think about scope, time, quality, and cost issues as well as risks that may concern their business unit or business processes that only they would know.

Once everyone is in the room together, lay down the ground rules:

- Keep interruptions to a minimum.

- Don't discount any idea.

- Critiquing ideas isn't part of the process.

- All participants have equal say.

- Think outside the box.

This process facilitates leapfrog ideas, which is exactly what you want. One participant mentions a risk event that triggers another participant's ideas, which triggers another, and so on it goes.

Brainstorming is useful when project participants work at the same location or are able to easily meet at a central location. The drawback to brainstorming is coordinating all those schedules and finding a meeting time that works for everyone. In addition, domineering group members can tend to squash the more timid group members. You may not get all the information in a group setting such as this because not everyone feels free to speak.

Nominal Group Technique

The Nominal Group technique is similar to brainstorming. The ground rules and the premise are the same, but the technique is slightly different.

Participants gather in a meeting room and are given a sticky pad of paper and markers or pens. The facilitator starts asking everyone to write the most significant risk they see on this project on the first slip of paper. The sticky notes are handed forward and posted on a whiteboard or flip chart. (You could post them by category of risk or type of risk.) The next question for the group is what's the next most significant risk you see on this project? The questions continue, and the notes are posted every round until everyone is out of ideas.

All the rules of brainstorming apply here. No critiquing or judging other's ideas is allowed. The main purpose is to get all the risks of the project fleshed out and written down.

This process works well for participants who are located together geographically. It allows for the discovery of a great deal of information in a short amount of time and eliminates some of the bias in the process because the ideas are written instead of spoken. Dominate team members in this setting don't have as great an opportunity to sway the group because they are writing their responses instead of talking.

Delphi Technique

The Delphi technique uses questionnaires aimed at participants who have project or subject matter expertise. The Delphi technique doesn't require a meeting (although it could be conducted that way if you want) and is ideal for those who do not have the time to participate in meetings but have special expertise or knowledge you want to access.

If you're acting as the facilitator of this process, you'll be the one to devise the questionnaire, distribute it, and tally the results. Back in our school days, we all hoped for multiple-choice tests, but this isn't the time for them. Questions should be posed in an open-ended format. You want the participant to generate information and knowledge without limiting their input.

You can distribute the questionnaires using e-mail or the company's intranet site. Once they're filled out and returned, you'll compile the results in a logical manner (by category of risk, for example). After you've put this report or list together, send it to the participants and ask for feedback. Now everyone who has participated in this process will get to see other comments, which may generate more ideas.

The Delphi technique is ideal for project participants who are not located together geographically or for those who find it difficult to set aside time for a meeting or an interview session. It eliminates bias in the process because participants are separated. Members have no pressure to sway them one way or another, because they're acting alone.

Status Meetings

Status meetings are ideal settings for uncovering new risks and reviewing the list of risks developed during this process.

You should consider setting aside a portion of each status meeting for risk review. This is the place to do the following:

- Access the life-cycle phase the project is in and the risks associated with those phases.

- Discuss the risks that have already occurred.

- Discuss the impacts of those risk events that have occurred.

- Review the risk plans, and determine if they're working.

- Determine if new risk events are possible as a result of past risks or response plans put into action.

- Open the meeting to discuss new risks not previously identified.

With all these techniques, make certain you put the right group of people together in the room. The processes will only be as good as the knowledge and participation level of the group.

Table 2.4 recaps the techniques and when to use them.

TABLE 2.4: Information-Gathering Techniques

TYPE	ADVANTAGES/DISADVANTAGES
Interviews	All projects benefit from interviewing experts during all life-cycle phases of the project.
Brainstorming	Good for group members who are located centrally. Members don't necessarily need extensive knowledge of the project. Domineering group members can sway the group or keep others from participating.

TABLE 2.4 CONTINUED: Information-Gathering Techniques

TYPE	ADVANTAGES/DISADVANTAGES
Nominal Group technique	Eliminates bias in the process, as all ideas are submitted in writing. Allows for a great amount of information gathering in a short amount of time. Not suitable for groups that are geographically separated.
Delphi technique	Good for group members who are not centrally located or don't have time to participate in meetings. Eliminates bias in the process, as no opinions are shared until the end. Time consuming for the facilitator to develop the questionnaire and compile results.
Status meeting	Ideal time to discuss risks, as many experts are present.

Diagramming Techniques

Diagramming techniques are useful for showing the logical steps in a process or a program, such as a flowchart, or for diagramming cause and effect. Ishikawa diagrams, for example, show the relationship between the effects of problems and their causes. These are also known as *fishbone* diagrams. Fishbone diagrams help you get at the root cause of problems or issues. Since your goal is to stay proactive, you want to identify risks before they become problems. Let's look at how the fishbone diagram can help you identify possible risk triggers.

The following illustration shows a fishbone diagram of a potential risk dealing with inadequate skills and training of key project team members. I've used the four project constraints as the categories for potential risk triggers, but you could use any categories that make sense for your project.

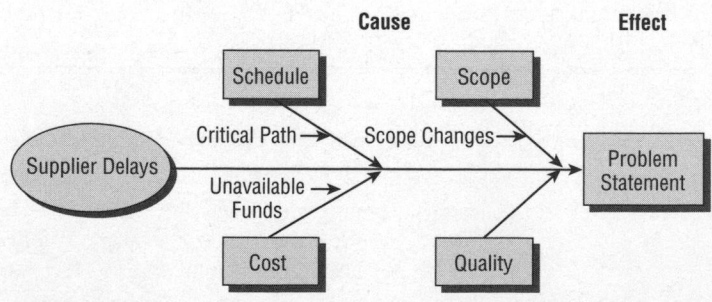

The idea here is to ask more of the what if…? questions. For example, what schedule issues could cause or create the inadequate skills or training risk event? One possible trigger is a critical path task that requires specialized skills. Since critical path tasks can't be changed without impacting the project schedule, you'll want to keep an eye on these tasks and assess the skills or training needed for the resources assigned to these tasks. Asking the same question of the cost category reveals that lack of funds would impact the availability of training for team members. Scope changes are another possible trigger as identified under the Scope category. This example illustration doesn't have much room, but the idea here is that you should ask what activities or events in this category could trigger this risk event? Use some of the information-gathering techniques you learned earlier in this chapter for identifying risk triggers as well.

Documenting Project Risk

You've done a lot of hard work so far. You've reviewed the project documents, put a bunch of people together in a room and convinced them to share everything they know or think about project risks, interviewed those who couldn't attend the meetings, and compiled a great list of potential risk events. It would be a shame to lose all that work, wouldn't it?

Identifying risks is half of the job—the other half is documenting them for easy reference throughout the project (and beyond). For example, when you're developing the project budget, it's helpful to know the risk events that are possible so that you can incorporate the costs for responding to those risks in the budget. And deliverables with a high probability of risk events occurring may need more time built into the schedule. Documenting also assures the risks aren't forgotten during the course of the project.

You also want to provide a way for folks to report new risks as they think of them. I'll cover creating a risk list and reporting new risks in the next sections.

Creating the List

Documenting risks serves at least two purposes. First, gathering and sorting the risks in a logical order will allow for easy review as you progress through the project. Status meetings are an example of where you could put this risk list into use. Second, the risk list can be useful on future projects that are similar in nature and scope to the project on which you're working. Instead of the new project team members having to start from ground zero, they can review the risks documented during this project and get a jump start on their risk identification activities.

The risk list itself isn't complicated. You can devise whatever method works best for you to list and document the project risks. At a minimum, I recommend the risk list contain at least the following information:

Identification or tracking number   This is a unique identifier for the risk. This number is especially useful if you've identified several risks and require several response plans. I recommend using a tracking number no matter how many risks you have. It's easier in a meeting setting to refer to "Risk 8" than to "The risk that talks about the network connectivity...no, not that one...the one where it talks about the switch...."

Risk   This is simply the name or type of risk event.

Description   This is a description of the risk with enough detail to determine the probability and impact. Or if the description is too long, include the location (or a link) where team members can find the risk description.

You could also add columns for risk category and risk type if you want to further classify the risks. Columns for life-cycle phases may also prove useful if you want reminders of where the risk events are likely to occur and during which phases the risk list should be revisited.

You can collect this information in spreadsheet format, in a database, or in a table in a word processing program. The database format has a lot of merit because it's easy to sort, it lends itself to categorization, and it's easy

to update. The project manager is usually the one responsible for main-
taining the list and keeping it current, reporting on the status of the risks
at status meetings, and closing out the risks.

NOTE   The risk list is your primary means for recording and updating
risk information as you progress through the project.

I'll build on this risk list in Chapter 5 by adding columns for impact,
probability, and risk score. You'll find a risk identification template on the
Sybex website at www.sybex.com.

Submitting New Risks

Since identifying risks is an ongoing process throughout the project, you
should have a formalized process for team members and project participants to submit new risks. All risks should be incorporated into the risk list
and examined later in the process for probability and impact.

The process for submitting new risks should be straightforward and
easy for the person reporting the risks. The key word here is *easy*—if the
process is cumbersome or difficult, you won't likely get many new reports.
Ideally, you should create a process that automatically updates the risk database when a new risk is submitted.

Short of that, you could use the Risk Submission template on the Sybex
website www.sybex.com and have the forms e-mailed to you (or a team
member) or posted on the intranet site with an e-mail notification.

The information you'll want folks to report includes the following:

- Risk name

- Description

- Potential impact

You'll want the team members who are reporting the risk to describe
the potential impact to the project so that you can analyze it and determine

if it needs a response plan. The folks reporting risks should think about impacts on the following:

- Business units
- Customers
- Costs
- Schedule
- Scope
- Other

Again, this isn't an exhaustive list, but it gets people thinking about several areas of risk impact.

Originators and Owners

Risk originators, as the name implies, are the folks who tell you and the team about new risks. This can occur in status meetings, in the hallway, or via the risk submission form.

Risk owners are responsible for tracking the risk, monitoring the project (and other events) for risk triggers, carrying out the risk response plan once the risk event occurs or is about to occur, and monitoring the effectiveness of the response plans.

NOTE The project manager isn't the owner of *all* the risks. This responsibility is shared among project participants, including the project manager.

The last thing you want to do is scare project participants away from reporting new risks by assigning them as the owner of the risk. Since they reported it, shouldn't they own it? No! The reason for that is the person who reported the risk may not be the correct person to assign as the owner of the risk. Risk owners monitor the project (and other events) for risk triggers and implement the risk response plan once the risk event occurs. For example, if a project participant who works at the front counter interfacing with customers all day reports a financial risk, someone from the accounting or finance team would likely make a better risk owner because they have the specific knowledge needed to address and monitor a financial risk. As the project manager, it's your job to help identify the person who has the knowledge and skills to handle the risk and assign them as the risk owner.

You'll want to make certain your project team participants understand the difference between risk originators and owners, so I've devised this formula you can share with them:

Risk originators ≠ Risk owners

Assure those who are reporting risks that they won't necessarily become the one responsible for following the risk and reporting on its status. This will create an open atmosphere and assure communication concerning risk events remains active and ongoing.

Checklist

The goal of this chapter was to develop a list of risks that you could easily review and build on throughout the remainder of the project. You followed along with me through several steps to reach that goal.

NOTE   Risk identification isn't a one-time process. It should occur throughout the life of the project.

Table 2.5 contains an easy reference checklist for the steps you should follow when performing risk identification.

TABLE 2.5: Risk Identification Checklist

ACTION ITEM	DESCRIPTION	COMPLETED
Examine historical information.	Review project planning documents and prior projects that are similar in scope and complexity to the current project.	

TABLE 2.5 CONTINUED: Risk Identification Checklist

ACTION ITEM	DESCRIPTION	COMPLETED
Review constraints.	Constraints restrict or dictate the actions of the project team and may have inherent risks associated with them.	
Perform assumptions analysis.	Review assumptions for validity.	
Determine risk categories.	Create risk categories, or use organization- or industry-defined categories.	
Perform information-gathering techniques.	Determine the best method for identifying risks, and conduct process.	
Document risks.	Document risks with an ID number, category, risk name, and description number.	

You'll use this risk list in later processes to analyze and prioritize risks and develop response plans, so keep it handy.

Case Study

Emily Lewis devised her risk list using the techniques she learned in this chapter. First, she and her team reviewed the goals of the project. The main goal is to purchase a new Customer Relationship Management (CRM) package that will perform at least the same functions as the current program performs. Second, they reviewed the critical success factors for this project. One of them states the new CRM package must interface with the existing Enterprise Resource Planning (ERP) system.

Further, they also reviewed the project budget, the work breakdown structure and project schedule, and the project's constraints. The driving constraint on this project is time. Bill Olsen, the CIO, wants this project completed by the end of the fiscal year, which is just shy of 11 months away.

Emily used brainstorming techniques and invited key project participants and stakeholders to the meeting, including representatives from customer care, representatives from information technology, a database analyst, someone from network operations, and the contractor working on the project. Two key stakeholders were unable to attend the brainstorming session, so Emily interviewed them separately (prior to the brainstorming session). It proved a good exercise because she was able to kick off the brainstorming session with the risks the two stakeholders identified.

Emily compiled her risk list, and Table 2.6 shows a partial sample of the list. Emily also assigned owners to most of the risks. The others require more research on her part to find the appropriate person to assign as owner.

Emily has decided to keep the list in a spreadsheet program on the project's intranet site so that everyone can access it. She also intends to set aside time at every project status meeting to review this list.

TABLE 2.6: Case Study Risk List

ID	CATEGORY	RISK	DESCRIPTION	OWNER
1	Technology	Interface	The CRM system may not interface with the ERP system.	Information technology
2	Data	Transfer of data	Accurate transfer of knowledge tree data from existing CRM to new CRM.	DBA
3	Data	Transfer of customer data	Accurate transfer of customer account information from existing CRM to new CRM.	DBA
4	Resources	Equipment	More equipment will be needed than identified in the project proposal.	Information technology
5	Human resources	Key personnel	Subject matter expert on the existing CRM system leaves prior to design of the new system.	
6	Project management	Project management	Project management processes aren't fully established.	Emily Lewis
7	Resources	Space	No space for additional servers and equipment.	
8	Data	Posting of data	Posting of data to existing and new customer accounts.	DBA

CHAPTER 3

Why Projects Fail—More Risks and How You Can Prevent Them

So far, you've learned the importance of defining a risk management plan, and you've looked at some techniques for identifying risk. I also discussed some of the common project risks that can occur on any project.

In keeping with the risk identification theme, this chapter will focus on risks that have more of an organizational or project management impact. These risks can be just as detrimental to your project as the specific risks identified in the previous chapter. Many times these risks are brewing just below the surface of your project. To keep the project from succumbing to one of them, you'll spend this chapter identifying their symptoms and causes so that you can see them coming before they jump out and yell, "Surprise!"

The PMINO Syndrome

Project managers, unfortunately, are sometimes nothing more than figureheads on a project. (And you thought the president was the only one who is a figurehead.) By that I mean they have no authority to make project decisions, assign tasks, take corrective action, or perform any of the other necessary activities project managers normally perform. The project managers are responsible for outcomes—translated, "You're the fall guy if this project isn't successful"—but are pushed aside when it comes time to make decisions and perform project management duties.

I call this the Project Manager in Name Only (PMINO) syndrome. Support groups are popping up all over the United States to help project managers cope with this syndrome—check your local listings to find one near you.

In all seriousness, this has the potential to be a project killer and a career killer. I'll talk about what you can do if you find yourself in this situation in several of the sections to come later in this chapter. For now, let's take a look at some of the symptoms of this syndrome. They are as follows:

- Accountability without authority

- Unclear expectations

- Executive managers who are micromanagers (the worst!)

- Meetings held without the project manager present

- Vendors run amok

- Lack of project management guidelines (what project management guidelines?)

- Scope creep

- Uncontrolled changes

I wish I could tell you the story in the "The Security Access Project" side-bar is simply a myth and that I've never seen this in action…but I have. It's happened to me, and it's happened to project managers I know and love. Let's spend a little time examining some of these symptoms more closely.

THE SECURITY ACCESS PROJECT

The big boss walks into your office. She starts out with a telltale line, "I think you're ready for some new challenges." You put your head in your hand and groan. If she only knew how many challenges you'd like taken off your plate right now…but that's another story. "I'm appointing you the project manager for our building security project. We'll be upgrading the external security access devices, but the biggest part of this project entails installing security access panels on the elevators and department entrances. It also requires building access control doors in areas where they don't exist today."

You nod your head in agreement as she continues. "You'll be working with Melissa from facilities management and Harry from information technology. Of course we've got a couple of vendors involved, too. You know—construction and revamping the elevators and such. I'm expecting you to run this show. The executive team wants this project completed within the next 90 days. Let me know if you need anything, and keep me updated on status."

The big boss leaves you on your own to gather requirements and write the scope statement. After getting sign-off on the project documents, you go back to your office and find an e-mail waiting. It's from one of the vendors working on the project. It appears that the big boss and the vendor have been meeting off-site every Thursday morning for coffee without including you. From the gist of the e-mail, you conclude that some important decisions have been made without you.

You've also found that the big boss expects you to bring every decision, large or small, to her to decide. She also wants to approve all project communication before you distribute it. And she's informed you that she will assign all project tasks to the appropriate personnel—no need for you to do that.

This scenario is a classic case of PMINO syndrome and is based on a true story. All the names and important details have been changed to protect the innocent.

Accountability and Authority

I wish I knew who coined the phrase accountability without authority. It's another classic. As the phrase implies, the buck stops at the project manager's desk.... However, when they have no authority to make decisions or impose consequences on project team members for their actions (or lack of action), accountability won't help them a bit. I'll start this section with some descriptions of accountability.

Accountability, in project management terms, concerns assuring that the project is completed to the satisfaction of the stakeholders, on time, and within budget. This means the project manager must assure all the project team members are working cooperatively toward completing the goals of the project and completing their tasks satisfactorily and on time. Think of accountability in this instance as a hierarchy, or tiered levels, of responsibility. The first tier concerns the overall success of the project—the project manager is solely responsible for this one. The second level of accountability belongs to team members who are responsible for completing their respective tasks. For example, in the previous sidebar example, Melissa is responsible for the facilities aspect of the project. She will coordinate with the elevator contractors and the building maintenance crew to install the new system. Harry is responsible for integrating the software that runs and monitors the security system into the corporate network. Each of these folks is accountable to the project manager for completing their tasks satisfactorily and on time. The accountability for this project looks like the following graphic.

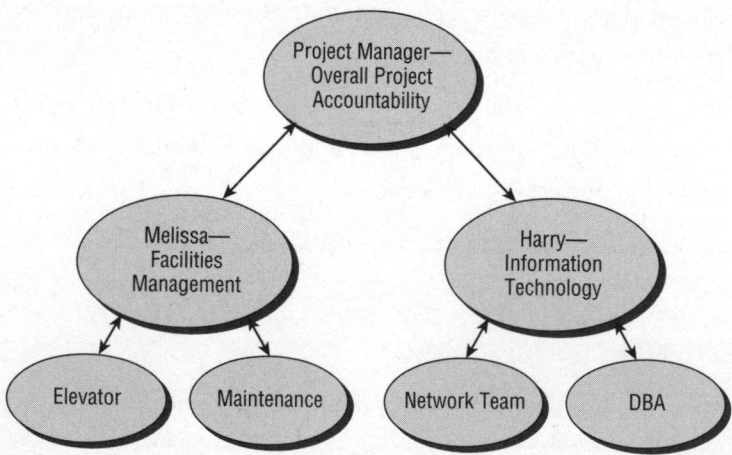

The project charter, which is a result of the Initiating life-cycle phase of the project, is where the project manager is identified and given the authority to begin the project. Authority means having the ability to make and enforce decisions and to administer consequences and rewards to team members for completing—or not completing—project tasks.

Authority consists of several elements, including the following:

- Making project decisions

- Assigning project tasks

- Choosing or recommending project team members

- Administering or recommending consequences for performance issues

- Removing team members from the project (or recommending their removal)

Regardless of the project, at a minimum the project manager should have authority for each of the items listed previously. What's important here is that you work with your manager or the executive sponsor in determining the amount of authority you'll have in each of these areas.

NOTE   I strongly recommend you meet with your project sponsor or manager prior to beginning the project to determine your level of authority for the project. You want to know up front what types of decisions you can make on your own without input and what the escalation process is.

For example, the project manager usually makes project decisions of a day-to-day nature. And I strongly recommend the project manager be given the authority to do so. Someone must be in charge of the everyday activities who is ready and willing to make decisions. Otherwise, every decision has to wait for the project manager to get with the project sponsor, who may have to consult with someone else, which can potentially cause serious delays. Also, the project sponsor doesn't have the benefit of the thorough level of knowledge the project manager has. I love a quote by David McCullough in his book *The Great Bridge: The Epic Story of the Building of the Brooklyn Bridge* (Simon & Schuster, 2001). On page 144, he quotes Col. Washington Roebling, who was the chief engineer on the Brooklyn Bridge project, as saying, "There must be someone at hand to say 'yes' or 'no'...and it often makes a great difference which word they use." His reasoning for this statement is explained right before this quote on the same page. "[Roebling knew] every day counted, when a dozen plans had to be gotten up and decided on without delay, contingencies considered, countless little details seen to and orders given, any of which might determine the whole course of events to follow." I couldn't have said it better myself: "any of which might determine the whole course of events to follow."

A person—usually the project manager—with intimate knowledge of the project must have the authority to make decisions to keep the project on track. At a minimum, they should have significant influence on the final decision maker because an incorrect decision made without the benefit of understanding the project as a whole could impact that event, which impacts another, and so on, like dominoes throughout the project.

Decisions are sometimes outside the realm of authority of the project manager's role. You should agree with the project sponsor on what types of decisions require their input or escalation. Perhaps you have the authority to sign invoices for amounts up to $7,500, for example, but invoices greater than this require management approval. Perhaps you may not have direct authority to remove troublesome team members from the project, but you can recommend their removal. In any case, make certain you communicate with your project sponsor or manager regarding the level of authority you have on the project.

NOTE Making a decision on your own that's later reversed by your sponsor because you didn't consult with them can harm your credibility with team members and stakeholders and cause them to lose confidence in you. Know your limits, and escalate decisions appropriately.

Creating Accountability

If you find yourself in a situation where you have accountability without authority, the first thing you should do is talk with your project sponsor. Clearly outline what decisions you have the authority to make and when you should escalate. Some of the things you should discuss include

- Project reporting structure
- Who writes and gives team member performance reviews
- Budget and purchasing approvals
- Who is the final tiebreaker (this is usually the sponsor)
- The process for choosing team members and who picks them
- How the project manager's authority levels are communicated to the project team

Since each project is unique, the amount or level of authority the project manager is granted may vary from project to project. Some of the elements that may determine the level of authority a project manager is given include

- Scope of the project
- Complexity of the project in relation to other projects the organization has undertaken
- Budget
- Project manager's experience with projects of similar scope and complexity
- Project team member's skills

Be prepared to discuss your past experiences heading up projects so that you and the sponsor can easily establish authority levels. For example, if you have past experience working on projects with large budgets or projects that involved multiple departments and vendors, tell the sponsor about that experience so you can put them at ease. Successful past experiences helps them establish boundaries for the current project.

When you're determining accountability levels for your team members, be certain to clearly specify their tasks and your expectations for completion of those tasks. Then monitor their work and provide feedback based on what you're seeing. If the work isn't up to standards, you'll need the authority to require corrections to their performance.

NOTE   Accountability and authority without the ability to impose consequences is like being able to bark but not bite.

Project managers need some teeth behind their bark. While I don't encourage biting your team members—never try this at home—you must have the ability to reward actions or impose consequences for actions. Consequences are the bite in this scenario. The ability to reward or disapprove an action sends the message that you indeed have the authority to hold folks accountable.

NOTE   If a project team member of yours knows that you, as the project manager, have no ability to impose consequences for completing tasks unsatisfactorily or for missing due dates, they may or may not choose to cooperate (depending on their motivations). If they choose not to cooperate and are unconcerned about due dates or the quality of their work, you suddenly have a project in danger.

Executive Champion

The executive sponsor of the project is typically someone in upper management who has the authority to approve the project and dedicate company resources to completing it. The project sponsor may also serve as the executive champion of the project. A champion rallies support from their peers in executive management and keeps them focused on the benefits of implementing the project. The champion is the visionary for the project, but the project manager shares this role. The project sponsor assigns the project manager to the project and is the one who should communicate the level of authority the project manager has to all the project participants.

While most project sponsors willingly delegate authority to the project manager, beware of the project sponsor who insists on being involved in every minute detail of the project. Micromanagers, at any level of the organization, rarely ever assign one ounce of authority to anyone else, project managers included. You'll know a micromanager when you see one because they make all the decisions, large and small, and you are not allowed to take any action on any issue without their input and go-ahead. I once reported to a micromanager who was so controlling I actually had to get permission before joining a project management users group during my own lunch hour! I'm sure you have horror stories of your own sponsors who've run amok. I could probably write a whole book on micromanager stories. But I digress. Do a little reference checking of your own regarding your project sponsor. Knowing what you're up against before going into it can help you devise a game plan. And a large part of that game plan consists of communicating expectations with them at the beginning of the project. I'll cover expectations of both the project sponsor and the project manager in the "Project Roles" section a little later in this chapter.

NOTE   If possible, and if it doesn't hurt your career by doing so, pass up the opportunity to head up a project when a micromanager is at the helm. Micromanagers not only burn themselves out, they burn out the project manager as well because you're forced to sit idly by and watch the project from the sidelines.

Keeper of the Risks

What does all this have to do with project risk? you may ask. Everything. As the project manager, you are the keeper of the risks. If your role has been undermined by an overly enthusiastic manager or sponsor, chances are they will ignore you when it comes to project risks as well.

NOTE Project sponsors aren't usually trained in project management techniques, and when project risks arise, they don't know to deal with them.

Time and again I have seen managers or project sponsors who ignore the project manager's role and not only drive the project into the ground but also drive talented folks out the door. There will be a time or two in your career where voting with your feet is your best option. Most professionals I know who pride themselves on their project management skills can't stand by and watch an otherwise viable project disintegrate in front of them because of the ineptness of management or the sponsor. When you've attempted to make your sponsor aware that the project is in danger because of the lack of project management disciplines and requested they give you the authority to administer consequences but they refuse, it may be time to leave. I've found myself in this situation a time or two and had to make the decision to find new employment where project management skills are valued and encouraged rather than squelched.

NOTE Project management is a discipline, much like the law, computer programming, or accounting, and smart project sponsors understand the value of having folks with these skills sets and knowledge running the project and watching out for risks.

Absentee Sponsor

Speaking from personal experience, an absentee project sponsor historically ranks as one of the top reasons for project failure. In the previous section I talked about sponsors who won't let you do your job. This section deals with sponsors who aren't active on the project.

An absentee project sponsor is a pretty obvious risk to spot. They don't attend status meetings, won't return phone calls or e-mails, and tell you they have other concerns on their plate that are much more important than your project. Although those issues are worrisome in and of themselves, the problems this causes can seriously impact the project. Some of the risks you face when a sponsor shows no interest in the project include

- Project failure
- Lack of timely decision making (leading to increased risks or project failure)
- Poor scope definition
- Lack of commitment from project team members
- Unclear expectations of the project and of the project team
- Limited stakeholder involvement
- Poor morale
- Uncontrolled changes
- Lack of funding

Any one of these risks alone can kill a project. But when they're all present because of a sponsor who doesn't want to participate, your project is likely headed for real trouble.

It's Your Job

Can you guess what one of the top reasons absentee project sponsors give for not taking part in the project? Drum roll, please...because they think it's your job to run the project. The project manager is responsible for all the ins and outs of completing the goals of the project. But when the sponsor holds little interest in their own role on the project...well, you've seen risks that can happen.

Since most of the time the project sponsor is a manager or executive in the organization, they think they have other tasks to do that are much more important than overseeing the project. After all, they tell you, they're busy people, and they believe the project is in capable hands. And it is. But that doesn't mean the sponsor should back out of participating in the project.

Now's a good time to look at some of the classic excuses and attitudes sponsors have for not participating on the project. Here they are:

- "Other projects and activities need my undivided attention."
- "The project manager is responsible for this project."
- "You don't need my input—make it happen without me."
- "I'm conflict averse."
- "I have personal agendas that are much more important than this project."
- "I'm only concerned with outcomes for the remainder of my time in this department or organization."

Although project sponsors may not vocalize some of these attitudes, if you know your sponsor at all, you'll know when these thoughts are prevalent. A conflict-averse sponsor, for example, typically refuses to make decisions and won't confront others when issues or actions need correction.

Sponsors mistakenly think because you're the expert that you don't need them active on the project. Although you are the expert, an absentee sponsor, as you saw in the previous section, is a serious risk to the project. So how do you go about winning the sponsor's participation? Good question. I'll answer it in the next section.

It's My Job

I can't stress enough the importance of communication. Early in the project, along with discussing the level of authority, you should also talk to your sponsor about their role on the project and the expectations you have about their level of involvement. However, you have to do more than simply communicate. You have to convince.

The art of influencing others is closely coupled with communication. The project sponsor isn't subject to your authority, so the only way you're going to convince them of the need for their participation on the project is by communicating with them and using influencing skills.

Influence is the ability to get people to do things they wouldn't ordinarily do without the use of force or coercion. You'll use influence with the sponsor, and others, to gain their cooperation in meeting the project goals, to lend support when needed, and to supply resources to the project.

NOTE   Those skillful at influence are generally more successful at gaining cooperation and are more respected than those folks who use force or authority to get the job done. Using a combination of your charming influencing skills along with a few well-placed facts should get you the results you want.

CONVINCING THE SPONSOR

"Ms. Sponsor," you say, "this document imaging project is a huge benefit to the organization. You can increase the retrieval of inventory records by more than a hundredfold. Imagine how well your department is going to perform once this project is implemented."

"Oh, I agree," Ms. Sponsor says. "But I don't have time to devote to this project. You and I have worked together before, and I trust you implicitly. Go out, and make-go."

"I appreciate your vote of confidence. But let me explain the value of your participation on this project. Other stakeholders, the project team, and executive management will be more willing to cooperate if they know you're involved on this project. You know this project also helps out the accounting department, and their participation is needed in a later phase."

Ms. Sponsor nods her head. You know you're making headway.

"I know we've worked together before, but let's take just a minute or two to go over each of our roles on the project and talk about expectations."

One key when using the influencing tool is to think about how the situation you need resolved will benefit the stakeholder or sponsor. When talking with project sponsor—or any other member of the executive team, for that matter—ask yourself, how does this benefit ___? Fill in the blank with your sponsor's name. Executives are always looking for ways to improve business processes, operate more efficiently, increase production, decrease errors, and so on. Find out how your stakeholder can benefit by helping you, and then actively communicate those benefits.

Project Roles

In addition to describing the benefits the sponsor will enjoy as a result of their participation on the project, it's also a good idea to discuss the role of the sponsor and the expectations you both have of each other throughout the project.

You should discuss the role of the sponsor in concrete terms. You'll want to state specifically the activities you're looking for the sponsor to fulfill. Some of the responsibilities of the executive sponsor in regard to the project include

- Appointing the project manager
- Communicating the project manager's level of authority to project team members
- Encouraging the use of proper project management techniques
- Serving as the tiebreaker on disputed issues
- Making decisions regarding project outcomes
- Providing funding and other resources
- Winning upper management support for the project
- Serving as a project advisor

- Removing obstacles and roadblocks too large for the project manager to handle on their own

- Serving on the project oversight committee

- Acting as project champion

Some of the decisions the project sponsor makes involve trade-offs among the project constraints. I talked about constraints in Chapter 2, "Identifying and Documenting Risks." Make certain you understand what the primary constraint of the project is. This will help you in future discussions with the project sponsor and when making recommendations to them regarding the action to take. For example, if time is the primary constraint and a risk occurs that has the potential to impact the project schedule, your recommendations on courses of action may include increasing the budget (to bring on more resources), decreasing project scope (to keep the schedule intact), or decreasing quality standards.

Regardless of the constraint, make certain whenever you approach the sponsor with a problem that you also have a recommended solution.

NOTE The project sponsor has the job of making tiebreaker decisions and resolving conflicts. However, the project sponsor isn't alone in this—recommended courses of action should come from you. When you present a problem to the sponsor, also present alternative courses of action and a recommended solution. Make certain you have the facts together, and check them beforehand. It's embarrassing to tell the sponsor one thing and then go back later and have to correct everything you said because you found out information you should have known when speaking to them the first time.

Last but not least, discuss the expectations you have of the sponsor throughout the project, and get a list of expectations they have of you. In keeping with the previous note, go into this with a few discussion points already in hand. I've outlined a few ideas regarding expectations of both the project sponsor and the project manager to give you a good start. Here are some PM expectations of the project sponsor:

Set clear expectations Establish meaningful, concise project goals. Publish a project charter that outlines these specifics.

Communicate authority Establish and communicate authority levels of the project manager to all project parties.

Clear the path of obstacles Remove roadblocks, assist the project manager in dealing with uncooperative vendors and stakeholders, and gain senior management buy-in of project goals.

Secure resources Establish a project budget, and assure availability of qualified resources.

Make decisions Make timely decisions (even when all the information isn't known). Work with the project manager to establish an escalation path for problems and issues.

Resolve conflicts Quickly resolve issues brought to their attention by the project manager. (Note that all conflicts should first be brought to the attention of the project manager.)

Keep in mind that while I've used the term *establish* in the previous outline several times, the project manager is likely the one who will do the actual work of establishing these procedures. The project sponsor will agree—or make suggestions—to your proposed procedures. Here are some project sponsor expectations of a PM:

Successful delivery of the project Satisfactorily meet the goals of the project on schedule and on budget.

Effective use of authority Administer consequences appropriately, maintain a customer service focus, and escalate issues appropriately.

Problem-solving and conflict-resolution skills Maintain an effective problem-solving skill set, and escalate irresolvable issues or those issues with a significant impact to the project.

Good communication Maintain open lines of communication, and keep the sponsor informed of project status.

Team building skills Establish and maintain a cooperative, motivated team. Keep the team focused on the goals of the project.

Liaison between sponsor and team Serve as the liaison between the project sponsor, stakeholders, management, and the project team. Impart the vision the project sponsor has for the project to the project team.

Remain flexibile Maintain flexibility—go with the flow, as the saying goes. Understand how and when to pick your battles.

When the Sponsor Leaves

Sponsors come and sponsors go. But an active, engaged project sponsor who leaves the organization in the midst of the project can be as equally devastating to the project as a disengaged sponsor. Will your project survive? That depends.

If the project was solely the sponsor's vision and baby, the project may not make it—especially if other stakeholders weren't really behind the project to start. Conversely, if the project was greatly supported with plenty of management backing, chances are the project will survive. It sounds fairly simple, but you and I both know lots of issues are at play here. So what does a project manager do?

My recommended game plan in this scenario includes

- Stay the course.

- Keep the team focused.

- Communicate, communicate, and communicate some more.

- Meet with key stakeholders.

- Be a pro.

I'll cover each of these actions more closely in the following sections. In the meantime, hold on for the ride. If your sponsor had a lot of power and was adept at the office politics game, you're going to see a lot of clawing and hissing going on until a new person settles into the position. Focus and pay attention to your project until that happens. Meanwhile, keep the team on track and focused on the project goals.

Stay the Course When a sponsor departs for greener pastures, your short-term action plan is to stay the course. You've made commitments, you have a schedule to keep, and project deliverables are coming due. Focus on meeting those deliverables and keeping your commitments. The last thing you want to do at this point is provide good reasons to the stakeholders to kill the project.

Delay any significant project decisions if at all possible until the new sponsor is named. If it's not possible to wait, I recommend meeting with the sponsor's manager or another stakeholder who is actively engaged on the project.

Keep the Team Focused Next, keep the team focused on the goals of the project. The project team will look to you for information about the status of the project, and make certain you share what you know (obviously, don't break confidences). They'll also watch your nonverbal clues. Your attitude, the inflection in your voice, changes in your behavior, and anything that gives them telltale signs regarding your thoughts on the project can lead to low morale and lots of unproductive time spent doing nothing but speculating.

Communicate, Communicate, and Communicate Some More During this transition period while you're waiting for a new sponsor, communicate with your team members so they don't jump to conclusions. I recommend you even lean toward over communicating. This is one of the best tools you have for keeping the team's morale up during this time.

Meet with Key Stakeholders Meet with other key stakeholders and your management team to determine the course of action. Sometimes, it will be evident who the next sponsor will be. If your project is well supported by management and is something most all the stakeholders agree on, it's only a matter of time before the next sponsor is named. I'll talk more about key stakeholders in the next section.

Be a Pro As mentioned earlier, if the sponsor who left was one of the only supporters of the project, it's likely the project will be terminated. If that happens, don't take it personally. Wrap up the project professionally. Document lessons learned, archive project information (you never know, it could be revived at a later date), and talk to your team members about their next assignments.

Key Stakeholders

Project sponsors are not the only ones who can play the part of a micromanager or do the disappearing act when it comes time for project participation. Key stakeholders are also important to the success of your project and may engage in the same behaviors.

During your discussion with the project sponsor, make certain to talk about the roles and responsibilities of the other key stakeholders. When key stakeholders are peers with the project sponsor, you're going to expect the sponsor to have some influence with them. But as I've cautioned in the past, don't leave this job solely up to the sponsor. Use your influencing and communication skills with stakeholders at appropriate times during the course of the project.

One more piece of prep work you can prepare prior to meeting with the sponsor is a roles and responsibility chart or matrix. Table 3.1 shows a sample roles and responsibility matrix for the Security Access project (highlighted earlier in "The Security Access Project" sidebar).

TABLE 3.1: Roles and Responsibility Matrix

ROLE	RESPONSIBILITY
Project sponsor	To make project go/no-go decisions, serve as tiebreaker, and provide funding and resources
Project manager	To develop project plans, manage project schedule, manage budget, and escalate appropriately
Facilities manager	To work with vendor to construct access doors, work with elevator vendor, serve as facilities subject matter expert, and make recommendations regarding project decisions

TABLE 3.1 CONTINUED: Roles and Responsibility Matrix

ROLE	RESPONSIBILITY
Information technology manager	To work with vendor to integrate systems, serve as subject matter expert regarding IT systems, and make recommendations regarding project decisions
Elevator vendor	To manage timeline and deliverables, escalate project issues to project manager, and work with facilities and IT to clarify equipment and software requirements

This sample doesn't cover every role or every responsibility, but it gives you an idea of what to prepare for discussing with the sponsor. You want the sponsor to understand all the roles on the project so that when problems or issues arise, you have a foundation already laid for who does what. For example, decision making is the responsibility of the project manager and project sponsor. However, all other parties are responsible for making recommendations about those decisions.

Disengaged Teams

You've seen what can happen when project managers have no authority and when project sponsors think they have better things to do with their time than focus on the project. Now let's turn your attention to disengaged team members.

Team members may (or may not) state a host of reasons for giving you less than their best on the project. Some are within their control; others aren't. The more common reasons I've seen include the following:

- Loyalty to functional managers
- Lack of policies and procedures
- Lack of trust in the project manager
- Don't believe in the goals of the project
- Overworked (too many conflicting duties and tasks on their plate)

- Personal issues
- Conflicts with other team members
- Wrong people, wrong time

Some of these issues are easy to spot and easy to fix. For example, team members who are overloaded with responsibilities may need help prioritizing their tasks or need you to off-load some of those duties to others. Team members who don't believe in the goals of the project will drag their feet when given assignments, gossip with other team members, or may withhold information. They may also be vocal about it and let you know they don't buy into the project. That's actually the easiest to deal with because you can address their concerns and hopefully win them over to your side.

Personal issues aren't necessarily easy to spot, but usually some telling signs exist. Team members may call in sick more frequently than usual or exhibit changes in their personality. For example, team members who are usually jovial and easygoing snap at other team members without reason or become extraordinarily quiet (or vocal).

A lack of trust in the project manager is another sticky problem. If the project manager is new to the job and hasn't worked with this team before, over time as the project manager consistently acts professionally and communicates with the team honestly and openly, the trust issue usually disappears. If time doesn't seem to resolve the problem, meet with each of the team members and ask for feedback. Then hold a meeting with the team as a whole, and ask them to put their cards on the table. When issues are brought to your attention, make certain you set straight any misunderstandings and correct the issues they pointed out that are within your control and ability to fix.

I'll cover other reasons for a lack of team member participation and the actions you can take in the following sections of this chapter.

NOTE   Regardless of the reason for a team member's disengagement, you'll want to get to the bottom of the issue right away. Bad attitudes spread like the common cold, and your best course of action is prevention.

As you may have guessed, disconnected team members can pose some of the same risks to the project that an absentee sponsor does. Disengaged team members, especially if you have more than one of them, can cause a lot of damage to the project if you aren't watching for the signs. The following are some of the risks and risk triggers. Even just one or two of these items together can cause the project to take a nosedive. Be on the lookout for these signs, especially when they're out of character for a particular person.

- Inaccurate estimates
- Missed deliverable dates
- Poor morale
- Poor quality
- Increased number of change requests
- Increased occurrence of risk events
- Overspending and wastefulness
- Uncooperativeness
- Unavailability (especially at critical times on the project)
- Lack of communication
- Improperly escalated issues

One last sign you should look for is activity without accomplishment. This is when people appear busy, even to the point of being harried, but nothing is getting done.

NOTE   Activity does not equal accomplishment.

Organizational Structures

Understanding the organizational structure you're working in helps you in several ways. You'll be able to identify key stakeholders, you'll know who reports to whom (this is sometimes key especially when office politics are at play on the project), and you'll also get a glimpse of the historical level of authority that project managers are given based on the nature of the organization.

There are three types of organizational structures.

- Functional

- Matrix

- Projectized

Let's briefly look at each.

Functional organizations are the most common form of structure in business. This is a traditional, hierarchical approach where reporting structures and types of work are clearly defined. For example, all accounting functions report to an accounting manager who reports to an executive manager.

The advantages of a functional organization include

- Functions are clearly separated.

- Specialty skills flourish.

- Employees have one supervisor.

- A clear chain of command exists.

The disadvantages of a functional organization include

- The project manager has little to no formal authority.

- Multiple projects compete for limited resources.

- Project team members are loyal to their functional manager.

As you can see, key stakeholders are easy to identify in this type of organization, and it's abundantly clear who does what. When you've got an issue to discuss, you know who to go to.

The two biggest downsides of this type of organization are that the project manager has a minimal amount of authority and project team members tend to remain loyal to their functional manager. I discussed earlier in this chapter how to address the authority problem. This approach will work, even in a functional organization, provided your sponsor backs you.

Loyalty problems can become an issue in this type of organization. Typically what will happen is you'll be "loaned" the resources from other functional areas to work on project tasks. The employee, however, knows their functional manager is the one who gives their performance review at the end of the year. Therefore, the priorities the functional manager has will almost always take precedence over the project tasks. When that happens, the schedule is in jeopardy, the potential for budget problems exists, and quality may suffer as well because employees aren't as dedicated to the project as they could be.

You're probably a step ahead of me on the solution to this one. As the project manager, you should have input to the employee's performance rating at review time. Again, this is something you'll want to establish up front with the sponsor when discussing levels of authority. The sponsor should work with their peers (who are other stakeholders on the project) to establish that you will be part of their review and how to coordinate the exchange.

A matrix organization is a hybrid organization. It's structured much like a functional organization in that marketing employees report to a marketing manager who reports to an executive. The twist in the matrix organization is that project managers also report to a program manager, who reports to an executive. The project managers have access to the resources in the functional areas (accounting, marketing, information technology, and so on). During the course of the project, employees report to at least two managers—a project manager and their functional manager. In an efficiently run matrix organization, the employee will report to the project manager for the course of the project (or until their duties are fulfilled) and then return to the functional unit when they're done.

Advantages of a matrix organization include

- Project mangers are free to focus on the work of the project.

- Project team is freed up from functional duties when working on the project.

- Employees are assured of continued employment when the project ends by returning to their functional group within the company.

Disadvantages of a matrix organization include

- Functional managers, especially in a weak-matrix organization, have a lot of power.

- Project manager may not be taken seriously.

- Employees may report to more than one project manager (in addition to their functional manager) if they are working on more than one project at a time.

It's possible and workable to create a matrix environment within a functional organization. In other words, you could ask the sponsor to allow you to establish a special project team whose sole responsibility is working on the project until the project is completed. You make arrangements with the functional managers to return these employees to their departments at the conclusion of the project. This way, you're able to focus on the work of the project, employees have no distractions or other duties competing for their attention, and loyalty issues dissipate.

Projectized organizations are not as common as functional organizations. The structure of a projectized organization, as its name implies, is project focused. All duties and functions revolve around projects. Consulting firms are usually projectized in that project team members are assigned to a client who has contracted them for a specific project.

Advantages of a projectized organization include

- Project managers have ultimate authority over the project.

- Supporting functions report to the project or program manager.

- Project managers have the ability to select resources.

- Loyalties are formed to the project, not a functional manager.

Disadvantages of a projectized organization include

- Employees may be out of work at the end of the project.

- Team members (especially those with specialized skills) may have idle time between project tasks.

NOTE   If you'd like more information on organizational structures pick up a copy of my *PMP: Project Management Professional Study Guide*, Second Edition (Sybex, 2004).

Lack of Processes

Project management processes are the foundation for all successful projects. In Chapter 1, "What Is Risk Management," I talked about developing a risk management plan that details your approach to planning and managing risk. Communication, change management, scheduling, budgeting, and scope planning and management are a few of the other aspects of project planning.

The Project Management Institute does an outstanding job of providing the framework for project management processes. But if you don't use the framework to develop your own processes, you'll be shooting in the dark as far as your project is concerned.

Clearly defined processes and procedures give your project team and stakeholders level ground from which to operate. For example, instead of wondering what to do when a risk trigger is present, they can use the process in place to inform the project manager of the event. If a process wasn't in place for this occurrence, the team member may ignore the risk trigger, thinking it's not important enough to report. Or they may think they'll be the one held responsible for monitoring the risk, and not wanting to take on more tasks, they won't report the trigger.

Team members who don't have a clearly defined escalation path or have difficulty communicating with the project manager may blow situations way out of proportion. I've witnessed projects with this problem. It can cause serious delays to the project and keep the project manager involved in nothing more than busywork trying to counter the group's "overthink." On one particular project I know of, the project team members compiled some inaccurate information and jumped right over the project manager's head and right over the sponsor's head to the director. Needless to say, the director wasn't involved in the details of this project like the project manager and sponsor were. By the time the director was brought up to speed, the project manager had spent weeks compiling information, meeting with the team members and the director, reviewing contracts, and reviewing original requirements, all to show that the project deliverables were indeed correct and satisfactorily completed. In the end, this activity caused the overall project a three-month delay.

Establishing project management guidelines and processes is essential for successful project communication. It provides a safety net for all team members. They know what to do and how to do it. They also know what to report and how to report it. And we all know that the more information you have, the better decisions you're able to make.

NOTE   I heard a great saying the other day: "Don't believe everything you think." This has a good lesson. When we're left to our own devices, most of us can dream up circumstances for our situation that are much more complicated in our heads than they are in reality. Established processes along with a good dose of open communication will prevent the tendency to overthink.

Speaking of better decisions reminds me of one last point I should cover. You won't always have complete information when making decisions. Sometimes you'll have to make decisions based on what you know at that point in time. Insufficient information does pose a risk to your project. But so does indecision. After you've examined everything you do know about the situation, it's better to make the decision and get on with it than cause delays to the project. Of course, sometimes no decision is the right decision. When you find yourself not able or willing to make a decision, seek advice from your project sponsor and other key stakeholders if appropriate. They'll help you weigh the facts and together make a decision or encourage you to wait.

In either case, my recommendation is that you document your assumptions and knowledge of the situation when you make your decision. That way, when things change later and the decision has to be changed or modified, everyone involved will understand—and remember—the reason for the first decision because you documented it.

Conflicts

Conflicts with other team members are usually very apparent. I recommend you deal with these issues head on and resolve them as quickly as possible.

The approach I use is simple and effective. First, speak with each of the parties individually and find out the core of the problem. Don't allow badgering or demeaning comments about the team member they're having a conflict with during this conversation—stick to the facts. Your goal here is to act as a mediator, get both sides to see the other's opinion, and reach some middle ground.

Second, the next step is a meeting with all the parties. State the problem or issue as you understand it, and get the parties talking. Keep the meeting focused and on track. Don't allow the discussion to stray to other topics. Ask each of the parties to recommend solutions. You may ask them to think about this before coming to the meeting so they're prepared when you meet and then bring them to consensus.

So what happens when they won't or can't reach consensus? If you can structure the project tasks such that these two parties don't require interaction and they're able to complete their own tasks satisfactorily, then give it a try. Monitor their progress; if you're happy with the results and they're happy not having to deal with each other, you're on the way.

If it isn't possible to limit their interaction, it's time for you to make some tough decisions. You can't compromise the success of the project by having team members at each other's throats. Chances are one, if not both of them, have to go. This is why you need the authority to remove or recommend the removal of team members. If both of these team members are essential to the project—they have specific skills or knowledge, for example, that can't be replaced with new team members—limit their interactions as much as possible and consider always having a third party present (you or another trusted team member) when they do have to interact.

Wrong People, Wrong Time

If I were allowed to write only one sentence in this section it would be this:
Available does not equal qualified.

When you're negotiating for resources on your project, make certain you get the resources with skill sets that match the qualifications needed for the activity. Henry may be available, for example, but Terri is the one with the knowledge and skill level needed to complete the tasks. Don't settle for Henry in this situation. Think of it this way: if you needed brain surgery but the only doctor available was a podiatrist, you'd probably opt to hold off and wait until the brain surgeon was available. If you can negotiate or work your project schedule around the availability of qualified resources, by all means do so. However, sometimes you may be forced to take a Henry over a Terri. In that case, try to get someone who has at least some required knowledge and skills, and be ready to provide them training to help bridge the gap.

WARNING Buyer beware! Sending critical project team members to training takes time and money. You may need to adjust the project schedule and the budget to allow for the employee to get up to speed. And once they're trained, you should also allow extra time in the schedule for them to assimilate this new knowledge or skill and become proficient at it.

Vendor Relationships

You say vendor, I say contractor…in reality I'm talking about any outside entities hired to help you meet the goals of the project. This could include vendors, meaning suppliers of goods or services, who supply the hardware or equipment needed to complete the project. It could also mean a consulting firm you've hired who supplies contract staff with specific skill sets to help complete the project. For the sake of clarity, I'll assume the term vendors and contractors are interchangeable.

The reason I'm talking about vendors here is because folks working on contract are as much a part of your team as your own project team members. And the risks to your project come in when vendors really aren't part of the project team. Here are a few of the situations that can cause this:

- Vendors take control of the project and squelch your project team's participation.

- The vendor and project team staffs aren't integrated.
- No escalation path is provided for the vendor to report issues.

If your company has hired a vendor to perform the project, it's imperative that a project manager be assigned from your organization who will act in an oversight role. The project manager from your team serves as a liaison between the vendor and the organization's staff and is responsible for making certain the vendor lives up to the terms of the contract. When the organization allows the vendor to take control of the project, strange things will go bump in the night. The vendor doesn't necessarily understand your core business or its nuances. As a result, they may make decisions that are contrary to company goals, business policies, and corporate culture.

The vendor has the best interest of...you guessed it, the vendor at heart—not your organization. That isn't to say that vendors don't go out of their way to work with you and do the best job they're capable of doing. But after all, they've taken on this project to make a profit.

Think about it this way: Who knows the state of your personal checkbook better than you? Does the bank have a better feel for your checkbook than you do? Sure, they know the balances and have a good idea of the kinds of transactions that occur within a given time period, but the bank is primarily concerned with whether enough money is in the account to cover all the checks you've written. You're more concerned with how the money gets there, how hard you've worked to earn it, and how best to put that money to use for you and your family's best interest. Although you and the bank may agree on some of these points, you're agreeing from opposite sides of the fence. The bank wants to make money on your money, and you want to put your money to the best use possible. The same is true with vendors. Always appoint a project manager for the organization who will keep the best interest of the organization at heart when completing the work of the project.

Sometimes you'll hire vendors with specific skills to augment your project team. Be certain you assimilate them into the project team as though they were employees. If you don't, the risk is the vendors and the project staff could work in opposition to one another or toward differing project goals. Conflicts could arise that drag out much longer than they would have if the team were united. You may also find that information is withheld and exchanged only out of necessity.

NOTE   Projects may fail simply because the right information didn't get to the right people at the right time.

The project team won't function at its best when there are two divided teams. To reach a state of high performance, vendors and project staff should work together as one team.

Just as the project team needs an escalation path to bring risks, risk triggers, and other issues to the attention of the project manager (and other stakeholders if needed), the vendor also needs an escalation path. As the project manager, you should define the policy for vendors to notify you of problems and issues and also provide them with a way to notify the sponsor if they think they're not getting responses from you.

Escalation is a two-way street. The vendor may inform you of a risk trigger and expect a response or decision from you on how to handle that trigger. If you don't get back to them, your nonresponse could put the project in jeopardy. The vendor needs a way to properly escalate to the project manager and to the management team or sponsor so that decisions are made in a timely manner and the communication lines remain open.

Case Study

Emily Lewis wants to make certain her level of authority is clearly established. While this project is larger and a little more complex than others she has experience with, Emily does have a successful track record and a crack project team. Susan Gilbert, vice president of client services, is the project sponsor.

"Susan," Emily says, "thanks for taking the time to meet with me. I've taken the liberty of typing up some bullet items for us to discuss regarding my authority level on this project and the escalation process."

"Great. That should save us some time."

"As you know, we've already got a highly skilled team of folks assigned to this project. And I appreciate you allowing me to help choose the team members. However, some issues here and there have crept up that I'd like to put an end to now by establishing my authority level for the project and the escalation policies for the team and the vendor. Here's the list of items we should discuss." Emily hands Susan the following list:

- Setting up decision levels and escalation
- Administering consequences
- Approving vendor deliverables
- Assigning project tasks to team members
- Having input on team members performance reviews
- Creating a project reporting structure
- Escalating decisions and project issues

Susan quickly scans the list. "Right off I can tell you that you are the one responsible for approving vendor deliverables, which includes signing off on all invoices less than $10,000, and assigning project tasks to team members. I also expect you to handle all the day-to-day type of decisions and escalate anything to me that you aren't sure of or have a question about."

"Okay, done."

"Tell me what your thoughts are about project-reporting structure," Susan says.

"We have team members on this project from several departments including facilities, information technology, accounting, and customer service, to name a few. Also, two vendors are involved. I believe it makes the most sense for all project team members to report to me for project tasks."

"You mean we should transfer all these employees to you?"

"No, and yes. Project team members should report to me for all their project tasks. A few of them work full time on the project, so they should report to me directly for the duration of their time on the project. Part-time team members will report to both me and their existing manager. I will have input on their performance reviews as far as project tasks are concerned. All their project tasks will be assigned by me, as you just mentioned, and I'll contribute to their performance reviews by rating their performance on these tasks," Emily says.

"I can see how the employees working full time on project tasks should report to you, but those with only a few tasks or who are working part-time? Why can't they continue reporting to their current manager?"

"One of the ways I can hold people accountable for completing their tasks on time and make certain their work is good quality is by having the ability to administer consequences and by contributing to their perform-ance reviews. Performance reviews, of course, are linked with compensa-tion, so by communicating my expectations regarding their tasks, we've linked their performance with compensation levels. And that's a powerful accountability tool."

"I see your point," Susan says. "There's a little more pressure on them to perform at their best if you're going to have a say in their rating. All right, I'll work with the executive team to help make this happen. Let's discuss this idea of consequences a little more, and I'd like to review the escalation policy you've drafted as well."

Emily continues to work with Susan to define and clarify her authority level on the project. She agrees to draft the e-mail that will come from Susan explaining the new reporting structure, Emily's authority level, and the escalation policy.

CHAPTER 4

Preventing Scope and Schedule Risks

Two remaining risks plague every project. They're scope and schedule risks. Scope defines elements such as the goals, deliverables, and requirements of the project. The risk problem rears its head when scope isn't well thought out, isn't documented, and most especially isn't agreed to by the stakeholders.

Schedule risks are associated with elements such as incorrect estimates, unqualified personnel, and lack of resources, to name a few.

In my opinion, the two most important elements of the project plan include scope and schedule. Wait, I have to take that back. Budget is an important element as well. But if you've done a good job planning, you'll know before you begin the work of the project if the budget is sufficient. The same isn't necessarily true for scope and schedule. In my experience, scope and schedule tend to undergo more fluctuations and change during the project than the budget does. This means you should also have a solid change management plan in place so that you can formally address the changes scope and schedule risks may pose to the project. And that leads us to the topic of this chapter, which is watching for and reducing scope and schedule risks.

Scope Risk

A scope statement, prepared during the project planning iteration, documents the project goals, deliverables, and requirements of the project. The scope statement, in theory, documents all the work of the project and is used as a baseline for future project decisions. When questions concerning what's included in the project—and what's not—come up, the scope statement is the document you use to find the answer.

Goals, deliverables, and requirements are different elements of the scope statement. I'll focus the discussion for the purposes of risk management primarily on requirements. However, just so we're all on the same page, you'll look at the definition for each.

Goals Project goals are the "what" of the entire project. They are the accomplishments you set out to achieve. Goals should be realistic, should be measurable, and should have a time element. They should also include criteria such as cost and quality measures. The goals don't describe how results will be achieved. This "how" is described in the project plan.

Deliverables Deliverables are an output that must be produced to bring the project to completion. Deliverables are usually tangible and can be measured or easily proved.

Requirements Requirements are the specifications of the deliverable. They describe the characteristics of the deliverable and may include elements such as dimension, ease of use, color, ingredients, and so on.

The project plan is the step-by-step approach that details how the goals of the project will be accomplished. The action steps of that plan are more easily determined after you've defined the requirements.

Suppose you're planning a wine party for a couple of dozen of your closest friends. You've set the date for the third Friday in September. The goal of the party is to bring good friends together, learn new facts about wine, and teach them a few basics about the art of wine tasting. Since you're a project manager, you decide to write a project plan for this wine party. Some of the deliverables of this project include the following:

- At least four varieties of wine, all from California
- Take-away information on wine-tasting techniques and the wines tasted at the party
- Finger foods
- Glasses and tags

Your next task is to determine the requirements that make up the deliverables. Here's where risk comes onto the scene in full force. Deliverables are relatively easy to spot. If you're having a wine party, you have to have wine, some finger food, and glasses to drink the wine. But requirements are a little tougher to define and thus pose more potential for risk.

Let's look at some of the requirements for the first deliverable: four wine varieties from California.

- All wines must be red.

- Varieties include Merlot, Shiraz, Cabernet Sauvignon, and Zinfandel.

- Each variety must be from a different vintner.

- All wines must be from the same vintage year.

Let's say you're planning this party with a close friend of yours. She takes a look at your requirements list and exclaims, "What are you thinking? All the wines don't have to be from the same vintage year. A good year for a Merlot isn't necessarily a good year for a Cabernet. We want our guests to like the wine, so we should pick the best wines from the best vintage year that stays within our budget of $25 a bottle or less."

You perform one of those long, movie-length blinks and turn on your heels to storm out. Your friend quickly apologizes and profusely exclaims she isn't a wine snob; she only has your friends best interests at heart. Okay—you buy that.

Now multiply this scenario times two or four or six friends. You can see that when you have a multitude of stakeholders involved, reaching consensus on requirements can be difficult. But not reaching consensus can be the death of your project. You must spend sufficient time defining the requirements of the project and getting as many stakeholders as feasible to participate in this exercise. And of course it goes without saying, you want to document the requirements so that everyone involved on the project knows what they are. Let's take a closer look at defining and documenting the project's deliverables and requirements next.

Defining Deliverables

You can see from the wine example in the previous section that deliverables aren't as clearly defined as they are when you see the list of requirements that goes with them. Suppose you had a stakeholder on this project that wasn't closely involved with it. The first deliverable says you'll serve four wine varieties from California at the party. This deliverable standing alone could be misconstrued. Maybe this stakeholder happens to be a white wine lover. When they see the deliverable listed without the requirements, they automatically jump to conclusions thinking that the wine served will be white. Uh-oh, big problem. A disconnect exists between this stakeholder and the rest of the project team. You all know you meant red wine; this stakeholder assumes you meant white.

NOTE   For more information on project planning, deliverables, and requirements, see *Project Manager's Spotlight on Planning* by Catherine Tomczyk (Harbor Light Press, 2005).

For the purposes of risk management, it's important to keep these pointers in mind when gathering requirements:

- Remember that requirements are the characteristics that describe the deliverable (it's easy to lose track of this one).

- Link requirements to the deliverables.

- Write them down.

- Don't assume everyone knows what you know about the project or the deliverable.

- Prioritize requirements by rank to assure that the requirements with the highest priority are the ones most likely to get completed.

A detailed list of requirements that are linked to their deliverables gives you a much better ability to manage change. As stated earlier, the scope statement becomes the baseline for future project decisions. Clearly defined requirements tell everyone exactly what they're going to get once the project is implemented. If changes are needed, they can easily be weighed against the original requirements to determine their need and impact. I'll talk more about change management in the section called "Change Management" later in this chapter.

Some other advantages of well-documented requirements include better estimates and a better ability to monitor the work and status of the project. As requirements are met and completed, deliverables are completed because requirements are the building blocks of deliverables. It's easier to monitor the work of the project when requirements are well defined. Both of these advantages—better estimates and closely monitored project status—work well to keep scheduling risks in check. And you want all the advantages you can get because advantages help keep risks at bay.

NOTE   Simply stated, well-defined, agreed-upon requirements reduce the risk of scope creep.

Measuring Requirements

Requirements, whenever possible, should be measurable. If it isn't possible to measure them, there needs to be some discernable way to know the requirement has been met. The same is true for deliverables.

Requirements may not be easily measured, but it's almost always possible to prove that the requirement is true, is false, or has been satisfied. For example, you can prove that the wine for your party is red by looking at it, smelling it, and tasting it. "Red" isn't a measurable requirement, but it's easily proven.

Measurable or provable criteria provide a way to determine successful completion or fulfillment of the requirement and ultimately the deliverable. It also provides a way to determine if risk events are likely to occur. Vague, unclear requirements are a sure guarantee of risks, including some like these:

- Stakeholder shock ("That isn't what we wanted," they exclaim)
- Unmet deliverables

- Schedule delays

- Increased costs

- Inaccurate estimates

Let's look at a fairly straightforward example. Remember our friend, Ned, the photojournalist? One of the deliverables for his photo-shoot project is photos of Paris (imagine that). To take the photos, he has to take his camera equipment with him. Therefore, one of the requirements for the photo shoot is transporting the camera equipment to Paris.

Okay, that's a great requirement—Ned must transport his camera equipment. But this requirement isn't precise enough, so we need to break it down further. So how about this: the camera cases should be hard-sided cases with protective cutouts inside the case that match the kind of equipment Ned's team uses. This requirement is easily measurable and verifiable. And having a specific requirement such as this one reduces the risk that Ned's team will end up with cases that won't work for their equipment. If the project plan is properly executed, they have time to order the cases, test them, and verify that everything fits prior to leaving for the trip. If the cases don't work, they also have sufficient time to return them and reorder the correct ones.

This may seem a rather obvious example, but what if one of the stakeholders on this project knows nothing at all about camera equipment? Bear with me on this one—maybe this stakeholder has never seen a camera. If that's so, how can they understand the requirements of this deliverable? And what will they do with the case when it's received? The answer to that requires documenting assumptions and making certain requirements are as well defined as possible.

Assumptions are events or actions believed to be true. Although it's a stretch to document the assumption that all stakeholders know what a camera is, you can see my point. It's better to document assumptions than assume everyone knows them.

Again, the camera equipment scenario is an extremely obvious example, but carry this out a few steps and you can see how one or two technical experts on a project may assume others know what they know and not take the time to define requirements correctly. When the project is implemented, stakeholders think they're getting red wine but they end up with white.

NOTE Mistakes are made and risks are greatly increased when the assumption is made that everyone knows what you (or others) are talking about. Stakeholders can make this mistake and so can team members and project managers. Take the time to define your requirements and document your assumptions about the requirements.

Critical Success Factors

Critical success factors are those requirements or deliverables that must be completed (and completed satisfactorily) to consider the project a success. Ned buying special cases for the camera equipment may not be a critical success factor for the project, but having up to date passports certainly is.

Critical success factors aren't necessarily more likely to have risk associated with them. However, since they're critical to the project, risks that involve or impact critical success factors can have a more significant impact—or benefit—than other risks. That's because if you don't complete the critical success components of the project, you won't have a successful project. Risks may prevent the completion of these important deliverables, so it's imperative to understand what the critical success factors are and the risks associated with them.

Obtaining Agreement

Obtaining agreement on the deliverables and requirements of the project is paramount to obtaining cooperation and participation from the stakeholders. It's easier to obtain agreement when requirements are measurable and clearly defined. As I've already discussed, comprehensive requirements assures better buy-in because the requirements are broken down to their lowest level. This assures everyone on the project understands the requirements;

if they don't, they have the opportunity to ask questions about them because they're documented and readily available.

NOTE   Scope definition, including detailed deliverables and requirements, is an area where you can reduce uncertainty. Defining requirements in such a way that eliminates vague and ambiguous meanings and providing stakeholders with a project plan that outlines the "what, when, and how" helps accomplish this.

Back to Reality

Now that I've finished talking about projects in the ideal world, let's get back to reality. All stakeholders aren't necessarily in favor of your project or want to see you succeed. Let's face it—projects bring about change, and change isn't always accepted.

Stakeholders who feel threatened by the project or the changes it will bring aren't likely to be supporters of your project. They may openly disagree with the goals of the project, or they may go along to get along while privately seething back in their offices. The stakeholders who tell you straight up about their feelings on the project are the easiest to work with. The ones seething behind your back are another story. Some of the symptoms you can watch for include

- Sabotage (albeit by the time this has occurred you're doing damage control instead of acting proactively)
- Agreement in meetings but reluctant to sign off on deliverables or requirements (especially those that benefit others)
- Won't assign staff members to the project or won't hold staff members accountable for their participation on the project
- Don't show up for meetings
- Won't contribute to discussions
- Don't participate on the project
- Refuse to make decisions

So how does a project manager counter these actions and keep stake-holders satisfied? You've heard this answer before, but it's the best one to start with—communication. Communication won't solve all your problems, but it will go a long way toward negotiating and collaborating with unco-operative stakeholders. Sometimes you'll find stakeholders are uncoopera-tive only because they don't have all the information or they have incorrect information. Getting the right information in their hands will help avert this problem before it begins.

NOTE Educating your stakeholders about project requirements, resources, roles and responsibilities, commitment levels, risks, and so on, will help gain their buy-in on the project and elimi-nate some of the potential for sabotage and lack of participation.

Stakeholders may also have ulterior motives—but don't tell them I told you that. Maybe they have projects they deem more important than the one on which you're working. If that's the case, it means they'll devote resources and energy to their own projects before they'll help with yours. That's understandable, but it puts your project at risk. Again, communi-cate the goals of the project and the benefits the stakeholder is likely to enjoy once it's implemented. This won't always win their favor, but all stakeholders like to know how you can make life easier for them. Another approach you can try is to negotiate for one of their senior staff members to fill their place on your project. If they truly are too involved in their own project, perhaps they could assign a senior staff member or someone else to your project.

Uncertainty

In the previous chapter, I talked about inadequate information. The reality is many project decisions are made in uncertainty. Time, cost, resources, and any number of important pieces of information are missing. Risk man-agement doesn't presume an ability to eliminate uncertainty; however, identifying and analyzing project risks will help the project manager and key stakeholders make better decisions. When you identify what can happen, how it can happen, and what the impacts are, you've reduced uncertainty because you've thought through the kinds of events that can impact the project.

DO STAKEHOLDERS GO TO KINDERGARTEN?

"I was told I would attend these status meetings and devote at least half of my time to this project," stakeholder Mr. Robbins laments. "But don't think that means I'm going to cooperate or help you in any way with this project. You all know that Amanda resigned last week, and I'm scrambling to keep Project Run-About on track. Taking on another project is the last thing I planned to do." Mr. Robbins rubs his chin and looks directly at you. "Seems someone got to Ms. Sponsor and told her I wasn't participating as much as needed on this project. Well, here I am. If you have decisions to make, my answer is no. Now let's get on with it so I can get back to my office and do some real work."

Mr. Robbins isn't a happy camper and unfortunately appears as though he skipped some lessons on tact and diplomacy back in kindergarten. But the good news is, you know what his problem is and you know what he's thinking. Take him out for a cup of coffee or lunch. Explain that you understand his frustrations and challenges. Offer to help him with Project Run-About in exchange for a higher commitment level to your project. If help from you or your team isn't possible, recommend a co-worker with solid experience or a consulting firm that can step in and help out. Make sure you squeeze in some of the benefits his department will see as a result of this project to help influence a more cooperative mood.

Let's use a personal example. Heaven forbid—you've received word your company is going to do a layoff. Talk about uncertainty. You don't know if your position is one of the ones targeted for layoff. If you do get laid off, you don't know how long it will take to find another job, you're not certain how or if you can keep making the mortgage payment, and given all the other stresses you're under right now, this just might be the icing on the cake that throws you over the edge into hysterical dementia. Will your insurance cover hospitalization? Will you have insurance? Will the dementia subside when you find a new job?

Now let's take the example from a risk management approach. Yes, all the answers to these questions are uncertain. However, you can play the "what if" game to think through each of one of them. What if your position is targeted? You can contact an employment placement firm, send out résumés on interesting jobs you find in the paper or the Internet, post your résumé on a job search site, call everyone you know to tell them you're looking for a new position, borrow money from your mom and dad to help make ends meet, sell the kids' toys (those electronic gadgets fetch some good prices on Internet auction sites), and so on. Each of these possibilities helps eliminate a tiny bit of uncertainty. You know what can happen, and you've devised a plan to deal with it. That's what risk management is all about.

Preventing Scope Creep

Scope creep, that slimy little green creature that eats your tomato plants...oh sorry, there are no tomatoes in this story. But tomato hornworms do remind of me scope creep, now that I think about it. Just like the tomato hornworm, scope creep slowly inches along the length of the project, not really drawing too much attention to itself until the next thing you know, a lot of damage is done. It's like walking out to the garden one day to find half the leaves on your tomato plants chewed away.

If you would have been monitoring your plants a little more closely, you may have seen some telltale signs of these creepy little culprits. Hornworms deposit tiny black squares of waste on the leaves of the plant. They like to hide on the underside of leaves and stems, and of course they're the same color as the tomato plants, so they're hard to see. They chew away at the leaves and leave ragged edges, rather than holes, as they progress. If you're monitoring the plants closely, turning back a few leaves now and then and examining the shoots, you may spot them before they make too much progress. Otherwise, all of sudden one day the leaves and the tender part of stems are gone!

In my experience, scope creep on projects happens the same way. Slowly over time so many changes are made that the project no longer resembles the original goals and plans. Scope creep is a project killer, and it's a risk that's ever present on any project. Let's look at some of the things that cause scope creep.

- Project manager's (or project team's) lack of understanding of the business functions and business processes of the key stakeholders departments
- Unidentified business areas or unidentified stakeholders that can impact the project
- Undocumented assumptions
- New requirements identified after the work of the project begins
- "Please, just one more change, no one will know"
- Uncontrolled change requests
- Inadequate change control processes

You, too, can prevent scope creep. (I just had to do say that.) Your first, and best, proactive response to scope creep is communication. Spending the time to document requirements will save you many headaches later when the work of the project begins and the change requests start flying.

NOTE   Some project managers play the "knowledge is power" game. They hoard information like it's a commodity. I urge you to refrain from this game at all costs. Other players know when you're actively engaged in this ploy, and they'll gladly join in. If you withhold what you know, and project team members withhold what they know, and stakeholders withhold what they know, you'll succeed in creating the perfect breeding ground for risks. This practice renders almost everyone incapable of making a good decision. Share information with others. Ask for their input and feedback, and make it a practice to lean toward overcommunicating. If you do, others will follow suit. The more information that's out in the open and known by the key players, the better decisions everyone will make.

Your next best proactive response is to practice good project management techniques. This includes sound project planning, risk management, and change management techniques, to name a few. I'll talk more about change management in a later section of this chapter called "Change Management."

The following list recaps the things I've covered that can help prevent scope creep:

- Requirements broken down to their lowest level
- Measurable or provable requirements
- Documented requirements
- Documented assumptions
- Documented critical success factors
- Stakeholder buy-in
- Documented policies and procedures
- Use of good project management techniques
- Use of change control processes

Schedule Risks

Once project schedule dates are published, stakeholders will hold you to it. Warning: failing to meet the published schedule dates kills your credibility with stakeholders. Stakeholders can be a pretty forgiving bunch, but when it comes to missed dates, suddenly you become unreliable and untrustworthy in their eyes.

I won't tell you that you can run projects without missing dates. The larger and more complex the project is, the higher likelihood you have of missing some dates. Again, the key is communication—especially when you know an important date is going to be missed. Tell them before the date slips that it's going to happen, not after it occurs. You can maintain your credibility and trust with the stakeholders by keeping them informed of project status, actively involving them in decisions that require their input, and consistently keeping your word—do what you say you're going to do.

You can do certain things to help minimize schedule risk (such as preparing accurate estimates), and I'll get to those shortly. First, though, I'll show you two examples of how schedules can become set in stone before you even realize it.

One scenario I've seen time and again works like this. Mr. Sponsor leans across the desk and says: "Now you have a general idea of what this project is all about. I realize you still have to dig out the details, but I think you can see what we're trying to accomplish. So how soon do you think you can have it done?" *Stop* right there. Don't commit to a date. At this point you're missing several key pieces of information, including the following:

- Detailed requirements
- Resource assignments and availability
- Budget
- Tasks (determined from the requirements)
- Project schedule (based on the requirements and tasks)

Even if this project is almost exactly like other projects you've done in the past and you can quickly assess the scope and tasks in your head, you'll do yourself a disservice by spitting out a date at this point in the discussion. Remember that while you're quickly scanning the database in your brain for how long a previous project like this took to complete, you're making a lot of assumptions without realizing it. Those assumptions need to be documented because they can and will change throughout the project and thereby impact the schedule.

Train your sponsors and stakeholders to know that you and your team have to work through the proper steps, determine the requirements, break down the tasks, and come up with some reliable estimates before you can determine a final completion date. I can promise that if you make up a date for this project during the initial conversations about the goals of the project, they're going to expect you to determine dates on the fly for all your projects. Stop schedule risk now—train your stakeholders well.

Another scenario I've seen as often as the first example is this one: "Project Manager, this project must be completed by the end of June, no exceptions. Any questions?"

"Yes," you're thinking but probably don't say it. This one is a little more difficult to address. The project date has been mandated from on high. The big boss says it will be so—therefore, it will be so. This scenario brings us back to the project constraints. It's obvious from this discussion that time is the primary driver on this project, and the date can't move. That means scope, budget, or quality will have to be modified to accommodate the schedule.

If scope is too large and complex given the timeframe you have to work with, consider breaking the project into phases. You'll have to ditch some of the nonpriority requirements to meet the date, so start now to prioritize the requirements. Include your stakeholders in the decision-making process or ask the sponsor to make the call on what's included in scope. You're going to need the help of the sponsor in this case because stakeholders will not willingly give up functionality they're expecting out of the project. Each one considers their requirement one of the most important of the project.

RACE CAR JUNCTURE

Project Webify is one of the most important projects this organization has ever undertaken. To assure its success, the project sponsor hires not one but three project managers to run the project. Ms. Sponsor brings in a cast of thousands to assist the existing staff with project tasks. The completion date is mandated, the scope can't change, and quality checks are required. One of the project managers is in charge of tracking schedule progress. He comes up with a clever idea. He lists the project's major milestones down the left side of a large poster board and draws timeline intervals across the board. He then places toy race cars at the appropriate timeline interval for each milestone to track their progress.

Two project team members hover over the poster in the hall.

"Why is the Database Design race car sitting there?" the first team member asks. "I turned in our unit's status report just yesterday. We're behind schedule, not ahead like this shows."

Scope can't be changed, you say? Then you'll have to give on quality or spend more money either to bring on contractors or to purchase components that you were planning on building. Remember back to the constraint figures in Chapter 2, "Identifying and Documenting Risks." When one constraint increases, the others have to decrease.

When none of the constraints are negotiable—watch out. You're headed for the deep end without a life jacket. Unfortunately, what tends to happen in this case is the project team begins to stretch the truth—Okay, downright lie—about the status of their tasks. They'll tell you they're right on schedule when in fact they're behind. They'll claim tasks are completed when really they aren't. It's a bad situation to put a team into, and as the project manager it's your duty to educate the sponsor and the stakeholders about proper project management principles and disciplines so your team isn't faced with this scenario. Explain the importance of understanding the requirements prior to establishing estimates. Explain that assumptions are made early in the project and that these can change later and require scope or schedule adjustments.

This sidebar describes a case where none of the constraints can give. Unfortunately, the project manager felt compelled to show the project on schedule, or even ahead of schedule, regardless of where the project really was. I never recommend you lie about project status—it will come back to haunt you (and likely get you canned). Always tell the truth, even if it isn't what they want to hear. If this project manager would have prepared a project plan that accurately showed the project schedule and then discussed the time constraint dilemma with the sponsor and a few key stakeholders, they probably could have all decided on some adjustments that would still satisfy the primary objectives of the project while meeting the mandated timeline.

Estimating Activities

The schedule consists of project tasks derived from the requirements and deliverables. Each task has its own estimate, and when you consider the tasks collectively—taking into account dependencies and such—you can determine the duration of the project. This means estimates are an important element of the project schedule because accurate task estimates will lead to an accurate project schedule.

As we've stated, well-documented requirements broken down to their lowest level of composition is one of the strategies you can use to develop accurate estimates. Is it easier for a team member to estimate this task, "Prepare new product brochure," or this one, "Prepare new product brochure on trifold paper and include photo numbers four through seven and the following headers"? The second requirement is more defined than the first (in fact, it can still be broken down further). A team member is much more likely to give an accurate estimate for producing the requirement as stated in the second statement than the first.

Duration or Effort?

Project management scheduling software allows you to record task estimates as either effort-based estimates or duration-based estimates. What's the difference?

Effort-driven estimates take into account the amount of time required to perform the task. If I asked for an effort-based estimate to paint my office for example, I might be told one painter will take four hours total including preparation work. If two painters were available, the work would take two hours.

Duration-based estimates take into account not only the time needed to perform the task but also the span of time it will take to complete the work. For example, if I asked the same painting question as before, I might be told it will take a day and half to get my office painted. The reason is it will take the painter four hours to paint and another 24 hours for the paint to dry and cure. The duration of the painting task is 28 hours—much different than the previous estimate. This kind of estimate is important if you have tasks to perform immediately after the painting. If the next task on your plan is hanging pictures, you couldn't perform it until the paint had dried and cured.

Which is better? It's a personal preference. For small-to-medium-sized projects I prefer duration-based estimates only because, typically, people will give you duration-based estimates—especially if the team members aren't 100 percent dedicated to the project and have functional duties on their plates with their project tasks. If I ask a team member how long will it take to create that new brochure, they might say the end of next week. In their head, they're taking into account all the other tasks on their plate. The effort to create the brochure might only be 32 hours, but given all their other priorities they know they can't have it completed before the end of next week.

PERT

Program Evaluation and Review Technique (PERT) happens to be my favorite estimating technique. The reason for that is PERT takes into consideration three estimates to come up with a weighted average—also known as an *expected value*—estimate. PERT estimates provide you with a range of possible estimates, including a probability for success. Expected value estimates reduce the probability of unrealistic deadlines unless the estimates are wildly off. I'll talk about that later in this section.

The three estimates you'll gather to perform a PERT analysis are

- Most likely
- Optimistic
- Pessimistic

The most likely estimate is the amount of time under normal circumstances it will take to complete the task. The optimistic estimate assumes the best possible circumstances and conditions exist to complete the task. The pessimistic assumes almost everything that can go wrong will go wrong (short of natural disaster and other force majeur issues).

Once you have the estimates, you'll plug them into the following formula to calculate the expected value:

$$(\text{Optimistic} + \text{Pessimistic} + (4 \times \text{Most Likely})) \div 6$$

The expected value gives you a 50 percent confidence factor that the task will be completed as calculated. Considering the schedule as a whole, that means half your tasks are going to come in ahead of schedule and half the tasks will come in behind schedule.

Let's say our painter give us an effort-based duration of three hours for optimistic, five hours for pessimistic, and four hours for most likely. The expected value is

$$(3 + 4 + (4 \times 5)) \div 6 = 4.5$$

We are 50 percent certain that the painting will be completed in 4.5 hours.

If you aren't comfortable with a 50 percent confidence factor, you can calculate the standard deviation of this estimate (the pessimistic estimate less the optimistic estimate divided by six) to determine higher confidences.

Add and subtract the standard deviations to the expected value to determine an estimate with a higher confidence factor. Here's the rule:

- 68 percent confidence level requires plus or minus one standard deviation.
- 95 percent confidence level requires plus or minus two standard deviations.
- 99 percent confidence level requires plus or minus three standard deviations.

So, putting all this into play for our painting example, here's what we come up with:

Standard deviation = $(5 - 3) \div 6 = .33$

- 68 percent confidence factor: Work will be completed within 4.17 and 4.83 hours
- 95 percent confidence factor: Work will be completed within 3.84 and 5.16 hours
- 99 percent confidence factor: Work will be completed within 3.51 and 5.49 hours

When you see a large gap between the optimistic and pessimistic estimates, your risk antennae should go up. A significant difference in these two estimates tells you the team member sees inherent risk in this activity. This is a great opportunity for you to discover what that risk is. And when risk is high, I recommend using the estimates derived at two or three standard deviations. It provides you a buffer of time to account for risk events. If the risks don't occur, you'll likely be ahead of schedule for those tasks, which could potentially buy you time on other tasks.

You should probably count on performing the estimating activities at least twice during the project unless the project is very small. The first estimate is completed during the Planning phase, and the second is performed in the Executing phase after the work of the project has begun. Remember that when risks occur or assumptions change, estimates may change as well. Be prepared to recalculate your estimates under these conditions as well.

Defining the Critical Path

The critical path is the longest full path on the project. Critical path tasks are those tasks that have zero float time. Float is found by determining the difference between the earliest and latest start dates and the earliest and latest finish dates of each task. The following illustration shows a network diagram of a project. Path A-B-D-E is the critical path, since the duration of the tasks on this path make up the longest full path on the project.

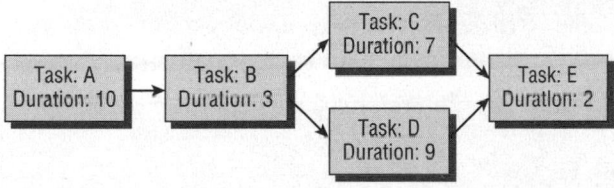

NOTE   It's beyond the scope of this book to go into detail on how to calculate the critical path. If you'd like more information, please take a look at my *PMP: Project Management Professional Study Guide*, Second Edition (Sybex, 2004).

Since critical path tasks have no float time, you'll want to monitor them closely throughout the work of the project. Schedule risk will occur if critical path tasks aren't completed on time. When you miss one critical path task due date, the entire schedule slips. Be aware that critical path tasks can change when assumptions change, so make certain to revisit your assumptions periodically throughout the project.

TIP   Noncritical path tasks can become critical path tasks when they use up all of their slack time. This may require a trip back through the estimating process and a redefinition of the critical path.

Again, communication is your friend. Keep stakeholders and project team members informed of changes to the schedule and the critical path. Monitor team member progress, and hold them accountable for providing you with accurate status reports. Pay particular attention to the status of critical path tasks, and be prepared to perform new estimates.

WARNING   Never tell your stakeholders the schedule has wiggle room. They'll want to know where it is and then either make you take it out or do the mental calculations to account for it and shift the due dates back. It's standard project management practice to provide a little breathing room (contingency time) in the schedule to account for uncertainties. The trick is keeping the breathing room estimates reasonable. The PERT method helps you do this.

The People Factor

If it weren't for people, we could complete all our projects on time, on schedule, and on budget. But then again, it takes people to perform the tasks on the project, so I'm afraid we're stuck with them.

As I've discussed, you're going to rely on your experienced team members to provide you with estimates so that you can develop a schedule. Believe it or not, some project managers don't think they need team member input—especially project managers who have previously performed the tasks themselves. Although using your own estimates as a sanity check is a good idea, not asking the team member who is responsible for the task to provide an estimate is foolish.

The benefits of involving team members in estimating activities works for you and your team members in several ways.

- Serves as a motivator.

- Holds them accountable.

- Gains their buy-in (because they had to come up with the estimate).

- Estimates are more realistic and accurate.

Motivated team members are typically productive team members. They've rallied around a goal, and they understand their role and the responsibility they have in completing project tasks. And they go at their tasks with a passion.

Motivation comes in many forms. One of which is allowing team members to have a say in how to accomplish the goals of the project. If you catch a micromanager at the water cooler, they will likely you tell you their employees aren't motivated. The reason for that is micromanagers don't allow their team members any creativity or say in how they'll complete their tasks. Professional-level employees particularly take offense with a project manager who defines every nuance of tasks. Give your team some breathing room. Assign them their tasks, and allow them to use their own methods to achieve completion and meet the deadlines. Of course, exceptional employees exist who require...let's just say increased coaching and motivation. New employees will also require a bit more coaching than experienced folks. My point here is to use a balanced, situational approach to motivating and managing your team members.

NOTE Unmotivated team members are a risk to the project schedule. Keep them motivated by recognizing their contributions. Give them meaningful assignments that will give them a sense of accomplishment or achievement upon completion. Provide them with opportunities to learn new skills. And by all means, solicit their input and thoughts on important project decisions.

Remember that all teams go through several stages of team formation. Ideally, you want your team to function at its highest level of performance. The synergy that's created by a high-performance team is almost unstoppable. And you can help feed that synergy by practicing exceptional leadership and motivational techniques with your team.

Change Management

Changes occur for many reasons, as you've seen throughout this chapter. The requirements change, the schedule changes, resources come and go, budgets are cut, and so on. Change management, including a plan and well-defined process, is important, because without it, scope creep could take over and morph the project into something different than when it started, or schedules could take on a life of their own—just to name a few examples.

Change, particularly uncontrolled change, is risky business for your project. But when change management and risk management are tightly coupled, risk consequences and impacts are reduced because you know what's coming and have an opportunity to identify new risks as a result of the change (or reexamine previously identified risks), analyze them, and develop plans to deal with them. If change is uncontrolled, we're back to our fire-fighting scenarios where focus is concentrated on the hot spots while smoldering embers go unnoticed out on the back 40 acres.

NOTE Scope changes almost always require changes to the project schedule and may require changes to the budget and quality plan as well. Budget changes almost always require changes to the scope, the schedule, the quality, or a combination of the three. Schedule changes almost always require changes to scope and may also require changes to the budget and quality plan.

Developing a Change Management Plan

The change management plan, like the risk management plan, is the road map for dealing with project change. It describes the policies and procedures used to manage change and how folks go about reporting change. It should also describe how change requests are reviewed and approved or denied. The characteristics of a good change management plan are

- Describes how change requests are submitted
- Details how change requests are researched and analyzed for impact to the project
- Describes the process for approving or denying the change request
- Describes where to obtain change request forms
- Details how responsibility for change request is assigned

You should publish the change management plan, documents, and change forms on your project's intranet site—or some other location easily accessible by project participants. It's great to have a process, but if you don't tell folks about it or where they can find the information, it's as good as not having one.

Assessing Change

Change requests must be evaluated for their impact to the project. Keep in mind that these impacts could bring about new risks not previously identified, or they could even represent a risk themselves. I recommend having a review period in each project status meeting where change requests and the risk list is reviewed and discussed. You may find that some of the change requests implemented will eliminate risks from the list or that you need to add some new ones.

Changes don't have to be implemented simply because they've been suggested. Remember that your scope statement is used in conjunction with change requests to determine how far from scope the change request is and the impact to the remainder of the requirements. As previously mentioned, keep a close eye on those scope changes because they impact so many other elements of the project: schedule, resources, budget, and quality. Don't be fooled into thinking that a scope change that doesn't have a price tag associated with it is free. Scope changes almost always impact the schedule. And when the schedule changes (positively or negatively), the budget is usually impacted as well. It may not be a noticeable budget impact, because you're not actually expending more money to implement the change. But you are expending staff time and putting off other tasks to a later date in order to implement the change. That means salaries and benefits are charged to the work of the project longer than originally planned. So, if you expand the schedule, you expand the budget.

NOTE If you'd like more information on change management processes, please pick up a copy of Claudia Baca's book in this series, *Project Manager's Spotlight on Change Management* (Harbor Light Press, 2005).

Case Study

Susan Gilbert is the vice president of client services and is a key stakeholder on this project. Emily is asking for Susan's assistance. Let's listen in as Emily starts off the conversation.

"The project team has completed the requirements definition for the project. I appreciate you loaning Neil to us to help out with this exercise. His input as a subject matter expert was invaluable."

"I'm glad to hear that," Susan says.

"Neil identified some requirements that we didn't know about at the beginning of the project because of his expertise. That helps us avert risk during the executing phase of this project. Now I'm working on creating a project schedule. Since Neil is well versed on the knowledge tree and other customer service functions, I was wondering if we could use him to help us come up with some estimates for tasks related to these requirements?"

"I'm not sure about that," Susan says. "I've got Neil booked for the next two weeks working with the marketing folks revising our client services training manual. I don't think I can free him up."

"Neil's definitely an expert, and I can see why you'd choose him for that role. As you know, this project is under a time constraint. The CRM system needs implemented prior to the release of our new billing system for transaction services."

Susan shakes her head. "Definitely. I can't afford to have my staff learning both a new billing system and a new CRM system at the same time. The people who will suffer for that are our customers. We can't let that happen."

"Then here's my dilemma. Without subject matter experts such as Neil to help us come up with accurate estimates, we're at risk for creating a project schedule that doesn't match reality. If the project schedule isn't as accurate as we can make it from the start, we'll likely miss important milestone dates and might have to end up cutting back on scope," Emily says.

"Oh, we can't have a system without a knowledge tree. That's absolutely critical to the success of this project."

"Yes, the knowledge tree is a critical success factor for this project, and Neil is just the person to help us estimate the tasks associated with transferring existing data and developing new data among others. If we don't estimate those tasks correctly, we could end up delaying implementation and end up impacting your client services staff with both the new billing system and CRM system at the same time. I agree with you that we don't want to frustrate our customers because our staff is overwhelmed with learning new systems. Having Neil assist us with these estimating activities will greatly reduce our risk of delaying the schedule."

"Emily, you've done a great job explaining the risks in this situation. I can clearly see the trade-offs, and delaying the new customer service training materials bears little impact to my area while implementing two new systems at the same time could leave us scrambling. How long do you think you'll need Neil so that I can inform marketing of his availability?"

CHAPTER 5

Analyzing and Prioritizing Risks

Now that you've identified risks to your project, it's time to analyze them and prioritize them. Not all risks need a response plan. Some risks may fall within a tolerance level that's acceptable to your organization. To determine which risks have the greatest impact to the project and which risks may not need response plans, you have to examine them and determine priorities. This chapter discusses the methods for analyzing risks, how to prioritize them, and how to determine those that need risk response plans.

Qualitative Risk Analysis

Qualitative Risk Analysis is concerned with discovering the probability of a risk event occurring and the impact the risk will have if it does occur. All risks have both probability and impact. You'll recall from Chapter 4, "Preventing Scope and Schedule Risks," that *probability* is the likelihood that a risk event will occur, and *impact* is the significance of the consequences of the risk event. Impact typically affects the following project elements:

- Schedule
- Budget
- Resources
- Deliverables
- Costs
- Quality
- Scope
- Performance

Of course, this isn't an all-inclusive list because any area of your project can suffer from the effects of a positive or negative risk. However, the areas listed previously are the most common places you'll see the effects of risk.

The probability that a risk will occur during the course of the project depends on the nature of the risk. For example, if you're planning an outdoor event in Seattle, Washington, the probability of rain is fairly high. If you're building a new restaurant in Phoenix, Arizona, the chances for snow during construction are low—so low, in fact, you probably wouldn't even consider assigning an impact for this risk.

NOTE   You should perform Qualitative Risk Analysis throughout the work of the project. This is the most common and probably the easiest method for analyzing risks for small-to-medium-sized projects.

You'll need some information handy to start this process, including the following:

- Risk management plan
- List of identified risks
- Current project status
- Scope statement
- List of documented assumptions
- Historical information

The first step in this process involves reviewing the project documentation listed previously. To analyze the risks, you'll want to understand what the project is trying to accomplish. It's also a good idea to review past projects of similar scope and complexity. If you have that data available, it will give you a good head start on determining the impacts of risks on the current project because you can see exactly what happened in the past and the significance of the impact (and how the team responded to the risk).

Qualitative Techniques

You can use several techniques when performing Qualitative Risk Analysis to determine the probability and impact of your risks, including the following:

- Brainstorming, interviewing, Delphi technique, and others discussed in Chapter 2, "Identifying and Documenting Risks"
- Historical data
- Strength, Weakness, Opportunity, and Threats (SWOT) analysis
- Risk rating scales

SWOT analysis is concerned more with the organization than the project itself. As the acronym implies, you'll examine the organization's strengths, weaknesses, opportunities, and threats. For example, if your organization has historically performed research and development projects with a high degree of success but projects concerning opening and equipping new labs have been not so successful, you can see that impacts of the risks associated with opening a new lab will have more consequence to the organization because it has historically failed at this. One of the other things this tells you is that you can minimize this risk by hiring consultants to assist in designing and equipping the lab.

NOTE I'll get into response plans in Chapter 6, "Defining Risk Response Plans."

One of the most common methods of performing Qualitative Risk Analysis involves risk impact and probability ratings or scales. I'll get into more detail on that in the next section.

Developing Rating Scales

Assigning probability and impacts to risks is a subjective exercise. You can help eliminate some of the subjectivity by developing rating scales that are agreed upon by the sponsor, project manager, and key team members. Some organizations, particularly those that have project management offices responsible for overseeing all projects, have scales already developed that you can use for your project. If your organization doesn't have them, never fear; I'll show you how to develop a set.

When you're charged with developing these scales from scratch, I recommend you include your most experienced project managers and team members in the exercise as well as the risk review board. You really don't want create these values by yourself. Additionally, you should get buy-in from the project sponsor once these rating scales are defined.

You have two ways to create rating scales. The first one I'll explain involves developing a simple High-Medium-Low scale. These values are known as *ordinal values*. Let's tackle the probability scales first. Table 5.1 shows a sample probability rating scale.

TABLE 5.1: Probability Scales

SCORE	DESCRIPTION	DEFINITION
High	Critical	Will occur frequently, has occurred on past projects, and conditions exist for it to recur
Medium	Significant	Will occur sometimes, has happened a minimal number of times on past projects, and conditions are somewhat likely for it to recur
Low	Negligible	Will not likely occur, has never occurred on past projects, and conditions don't exist for it to recur

These examples are somewhat generic, but you get the idea. You can modify these definitions easily based on your organization and the types of projects on which you work.

Now let's do the same thing for impact. Table 5.2 shows a sample impact rating scale.

TABLE 5.2: Risk Impact Scales

SCORE	DESCRIPTION	DEFINITION
High	Critical	A consequence that will cause loss, cause severe interruptions to the customer, or severely delay the completion of a major deliverable
Medium	Significant	A consequence that may cause loss, may cause annoying interruptions to the customer, or delay the completion of a major deliverable
Low	Negligible	A consequence that may cause minimal loss, cause minimal interruption to the customer, or cause minimal delay to the completion of a major deliverable

You aren't stuck with one set of scales for all risks. Most risks will typically impact cost, time, quality, or scope at a minimum. You could devise scales for each of these constraints and combine them into a table like Table 5.3. You can easily develop the same type of matrix for probability values.

TABLE 5.3: Risk Impact Rating Matrix

CONSTRAINT	LOW	MEDIUM	HIGH
Cost	Less than 5% increase	6–25% increase	Greater than 25% increase
Time	Less than 5% increase	6–20% increase	Greater than 20% increase
Quality	Fewer than 2 failures	3–8 failures	Greater than 8 failures
Scope	Insignificant change	Change to major deliverable	Change to a critical path task

These scales provide a way for everyone working on the project to describe risk probability and impact the same way. If you didn't have common definitions, their meanings would become purely subjective, without anything to support them. I could say a certain risk has a medium potential for occurring and carries a severe impact, and you could interpret that to mean it isn't important enough to deal with right now, so you'll cross that bridge when you get there.

Using the Scales

So, how do you use these scales? As I stated in an earlier section, you'll want to review the project documentation to have a solid understanding of what the project is trying to accomplish—that is, what the goals of the project are. Then, you'll go through your risk list one by one and determine both the probability is of it occurring and its impact. Let's examine the risk of losing a key employee as an example.

Probability asks, what's the chance of this event occurring? Let's say the project manager knows this employee well. The project manager knows this employee is happy with their job and very enthusiastic about the project. Therefore, I'd assign a probability of Low for this risk based on the definition in Table 5.1.

Impact is a different story. This key employee is the only employee on the team who has the knowledge and skills to complete some of the critical tasks for this project. Therefore, I would assign an impact rating of High based on the description in Table 5.2. If you lost this employee, it would severely delay the completion of a major deliverable.

So the risk score for loss of this key employee is Low-High. You'll use this score a little later, in the "Determining Risks That Need Response Plans" section of this chapter, to determine risk ranking and to determine if the risk requires a response plan.

Don't forget to document your assumptions. Assumptions can and will change, and when they do, they require you to reevaluate the risk for probability and impact. The assumptions you made regarding the loss of key employee risk are as follows:

- The employee is the only one with the skills and knowledge to complete critical tasks.

- The employee is content with their job, is content with their work environment, and is enthusiastic about the project.

Suppose your assumption about the employee's contentedness changes when you learn the employee's spouse has landed a new job in another part of the country making three times their current salary. Chances are fairly high your employee plans on moving with their spouse, which changes the probability of this event occurring. I'd reassign this score to High given this new information. That changes the risk score to High-High. You can guess, even before reading the "Risk Ranking" section later in this chapter, that a risk with a High-High score needs some attention.

Risk Lists

To give you a jump start on determining risk impacts, I've taken the list of common project risks from Chapter 2 and given you some of their possible impacts in Table 5.4. You can use this table or derive one of your own as a quick reference for risk identification and their possible impacts. One more tip: you could add a column to this table that describes the category of risk (I talked about that in Chapter 2 as well) for easy classification into your risk database.

Risk Tolerance Levels

Another tool that will help define risk impact is to determine risk tolerance levels. *Risk tolerance* is the comfort level you or the organization has for risks. Suppose you're a 275-pound brute who is surrounded by three bodyguards of equal proportion everywhere you go. Chances are, walking down a dark alley in the middle of the night doesn't faze you in the least. That means your risk tolerance for this activity is High. However, if you're a petite 90-pounder without benefit of bodyguards or karate lessons, performing this same activity may give you cause for concern. Your risk tolerance is Low, meaning you wouldn't likely do this activity. The higher your tolerance for risk, the more you're willing to take on risks and their consequences.

TABLE 5.4: Possible Risk Impacts

TYPE OF RISK	DESCRIPTION	POSSIBLE IMPACTS
Loss of key employee	The key project team member leaves and takes knowledge of the project, special skills, expertise, or process knowledge with them.	May result in increased costs and schedule delays. May result in sabotage, lost revenue, and erosion of customer base if information is taken to competitors. May also affect team morale.
Financial	Costs associated with the project, poor return on investment, inadequate project budgets, cost overruns, funding cuts, and stock market influences.	May result in project termination, extensive scope changes, extensive schedule changes, and poor quality.
Environmental	Risks associated with manufacturing, construction, or pharmaceuticals, for example, may pose environmental threats.	May result in financial loss, legal action, governmental intervention, increased cost, and project termination.
Stakeholder consensus	Stakeholders don't reach consensus on project decisions.	May result in project termination, extensive scope and schedule changes, may impact customer satisfaction or goals. May result in loss of revenue and customers.
Weather, civil unrest, terrorist acts	Risks external to the organization may often be unknown risks that could prove catastrophic to the project as well as the organization.	May result in project termination and increased costs.
Labor force issues	Strikes or work stoppages.	May cause project termination, schedule delays, poor quality, and increased costs.

TABLE 5.4 CONTINUED: Possible Risk Impacts

TYPE OF RISK	DESCRIPTION	POSSIBLE IMPACTS
Technical	Risks associated with unproven technology, complex technology, or changes to the technology during the course of the project. Performance risks include unrealistic performance goals, and unreasonable or immeasurable performance standards.	May result in increased budget, extensive schedule delays, loss of key project team members, failure to meet the project's quality goals, and project termination.
Management turnover	Changes in key stakeholders.	May result in project termination, reduced budgets, changes to or reduction of scope, inadequate change control measures, and poor quality assurance.
Lack of sponsorship involvement	Project sponsor doesn't take an active role in the project.	May result in schedule delays, project termination, inability to approve scope changes, inability to gain approval of project deliverables, and inadequate controls on the change processes.
Loss of project sponsor	Losing the project sponsor is usually detrimental to the project.	May result in project termination, schedule delays, extensive scope changes, and inability to reach consensus regarding project issues.
Change in ownership	Changes in ownership are usually detrimental to the project.	May cause project termination, schedule delays, scope changes, and cost changes.
Changes to current business processes	New projects often bring about business process change. People resist change when they're not trained or informed about the change.	May result in the project failing, increased costs, and schedule delays. Quality may also be affected as people discount the new features the project introduces and complain to management of inefficiencies or decreased productivity.

TABLE 5.4 CONTINUED: Possible Risk Impacts

TYPE OF RISK	DESCRIPTION	POSSIBLE IMPACTS
Cyclical	Risks associated with seasonal sales, for example. May include external cyclical risks that could affect the business, such as hurricane season or tourist seasons.	May result in project termination, schedule delays, and increased costs.
Availability of business or technical experts	Business or technical experts are unavailable to participate in the project.	May result in extensive scope changes, increased costs, schedule delays, project termination, and poor quality.
Reporting structure of the project team	Project team members reporting to both a project manager and a functional manager.	May result in schedule delays, scope changes, inability to meet quality specifications, increased costs, inability to control change processes, improper planning, inaccurate time or resource estimates, and decreased productivity.
Unrealistic scope, time, or quality objectives	Scope, time, or quality objectives could be unrealistic given the organization's resources and structure.	May result in schedule delays, project termination, increased costs, poor quality performance, inadequate change control processes, and inaccurate estimates.
Project team diversity, international projects	Cultural barriers because of projects performed in cultural surroundings the team isn't familiar with.	May cause schedule delays, scope changes, inaccurate human resource estimates, inaccurate materials estimates, improper planning, increased costs, inadequate quality assurance, and poor quality control.

TABLE 5.4 CONTINUED: Possible Risk Impacts

TYPE OF RISK	DESCRIPTION	POSSIBLE IMPACTS
Loss of company data	Theft of customer information, employee information, intellectual property, financial records, customer lists, competitor information, research and development findings, and so on.	Loss of company data could result in catastrophic losses to the organization in the form of lawsuits, lost revenues, lost market position, and irreversible damage to the company's reputation.
Skills of project team members	Project team members don't have the skills required to complete deliverables or don't have sufficient training for the complexity, size, or technical aspects of the project.	May result in project termination, schedule delays, cost increases, inaccurate human resource estimates, inaccurate materials estimates, improper planning, decreased productivity, and a substantial increase in change requests.
Skills of the project manager	Project manager isn't experienced with the complexity, size, or technical aspects of the project.	May result in project termination, schedule delays, cost increases, poor project planning, inaccurate estimates, and loss of key project team members.
Skills of business users	Project manager isn't experienced with the complexity, size, or technical aspects of the project.	May result in project termination, schedule delays, cost increases, inaccurate estimates, decreased productivity, and loss of key project team members.
Contract and procurement	Inability of vendor to produce deliverables, lack of skills or resources, and financial stability.	May cause increased costs, schedule delays, project termination, improper planning, and improper controls.

TABLE 5.4 CONTINUED: Possible Risk Impacts

TYPE OF RISK	DESCRIPTION	POSSIBLE IMPACTS
Scope	Inadequate definition of deliverables, lack of stakeholder buy-in, conflicting goals, and scope of greater complexity than previous projects.	May result in schedule delays, cost increases, inaccurate estimates, significant change requests, decreased productivity, and project termination.
Quality	Lack of a quality plan, poor performance measures, poor quality assurance, poor workmanship, and substandard materials.	Could result in increased cost, scope changes, schedule delays, and project terminations.
Schedule	Inadequate duration estimates, critical path not identified or incorrectly identified, availability of materials, and task dependencies.	May result in scope changes, cost increases, poor quality, and project termination.

THE CONTINUING PHOTO-SHOOT SAGA WITH NED AND THE GANG

"I don't care if it gets me arrested," Ned exclaims. "I need that photo, and I'll do anything it takes to get it."

Sherry, the project manager for Ned's project, is getting a little frustrated with Ned's antics. First he loses his passport, then he all but cusses out a baggage attendant. And now this.

"Ned, if you get arrested taking that photo, how will we finish the project? Have you thought of that? We have four days of shooting left after today. It could take me that long to bail you out. I don't think the magazine is going to be crazy about extending our stay another five days to account for the lost work, either. Besides that, we're up against a deadline on this project, and there isn't room for scheduling errors. Now, what will it be? Finish the shoot, or get this shot at all costs?"

Ned's tolerance for risk is obviously high. Sherry, being the good project manager that she is, communicates the pros and cons of Ned's actions. Ned determines that the risk of missing the rest of the photo shoot would be more painful than the benefits of getting this one shot, so he decides to side with Sherry's decision.

Organizations also have levels of risk tolerance. Some organizations are more risk averse than others. What one organization considers low risk may be huge to another. You and your team will have to do some investigating on risk tolerance levels for your organization. This will help you in assigning risk impacts. For example, if you know your organization has little tolerance for losing money on investments, then investment in new technology would have a higher cost impact than normal because the company has a low tolerance for losing money on investments.

Understanding past project successes and failures will help you get a handle on risk tolerance. Also, the risk tolerance levels of individual stakeholders will give you some clues as to the organization's level of comfort. I once had a key stakeholder who was so risk averse he wouldn't make decisions about anything. Instead, he'd let the chips fall where they may (which usually meant another stakeholder stepped in to direct things or the project manager made a decision on the stakeholder's behalf) and then took credit when the outcome was good and pointed the finger at the project manager when things didn't work out well.

Take the time to understand your organization and your stakeholder's risk tolerance levels so that you can develop probability and impact scales that accurately reflect the organization's level for risk.

Quantitative Risk Analysis

The second way you can create these risk scales is to assign not only High-Medium-Low values but also assign numeric values to both probability and impact so that you can calculate an overall risk score. This method is known as *Quantitative Risk Analysis* because you're quantifying the probability and impact by assigning a numeric value to each. This is my preferred method of determining and assigning risk scores.

Cardinal scale values are numbers expressed between 0 and 1.0. Probability is usually expressed as a cardinal value. The coin toss is a classic example. You have a 50 percent chance of the coin coming up heads. This means there is also a 50 percent chance of the coin coming up tails (or a 50 percent chance of it not coming up heads, if you prefer to look at it that way). If the weather forecaster predicts a 30 percent chance of rain, obviously there's a 70 percent chance it won't rain. The idea is that you can come up with an overall numeric value for a risk event. This score is known as *expected value*. Then you'll determine what, if anything, you should plan for based on that expected value. The risk score will also help you prioritize the risks.

Tables 5.5 and 5.6 are just like Tables 5.1 and 5.2 only I've added a risk value for the High-Medium-Low categories. Use the same group of folks that helped develop the risk scales to determine the percentages that should be assigned to each category.

TABLE 5.5: Probability Scales

SCORE	DESCRIPTION	DEFINITION
HIGH		
.80	Critical	Will occur frequently, has occurred on past projects, and conditions exist for it to recur
Medium		
.50	Significant	Will occur sometimes, has happened a minimal number of times on past projects, and conditions are somewhat likely for it to recur
Low		
.10	Negligible	Will not likely occur, has never occurred on past projects, and conditions don't exist for it to recur

TABLE 5.6: Risk Impact Scales

SCORE	DESCRIPTION	DEFINITION
HIGH		
.80	Critical	A consequence that will cause loss, cause severe interruptions to the customer, or severely delay the completion of a major deliverable
Medium		
.50	Significant	A consequence that may cause loss, may cause annoying interruptions to the customer, or delay the completion of a major deliverable
Low		
.10	Negligible	A consequence that may cause minimal loss, cause minimal interruption to the customer, or cause minimal delay to the completion of a major deliverable

If you want even more precision, you could create more than three values for probability and impact. For example, you might come up with values that look like this:

High-High: .80

High: .60

Medium: .40

Low: .20

Low-Low: .05

This gives you more precision and better definition between risks. If you have more than two risks that have the same score—for example, High-Medium—it calls for a little more subjectivity to determine which one is more important on the ranking scale. For very small projects, the three-point scale works fines. When you get into more complex projects, consider using the five-point scale.

NOTE You could forgo the High-Medium-Low value and use a straight percentage value. In my experience, however, I've found people are usually more comfortable assigning a High-Medium-Low score to a risk than a numeric value.

Calculating Risk Scores

You can record the final risk scores in two ways. You could devise a table and list the risk identification number, the risk, the probability, and the impact as individual components. It would look something like this:

ID	Risk	Probability	Impact
1	Loss of key employee	.10	.80

Or you could calculate a total risk score by multiplying the probability of the risk event by the impact. Using the loss of key employee as an example, you see this risk has a low probability of occurring but a high impact. Therefore, you come up with .10 × .80 for a final value, also known as an *expected value*, of .08.

Great...terrific. What does that mean?

When you use this method to determine an expected value, it requires one more step. You have to convert the expected value to an overall value. You could use High-Medium-Low, Critical-Significant-Negligible, or something similar. Your team must determine the range of scores that make up these values. An example is as follows:

Expected Value	Value
0.64–0.25	Critical
0.24–0.05	Significant
0.04–0	Negligible

Using the earlier example, you'd assign the loss of a key employee a final value of "significant" based on where the risk score falls within the range. As you'll see when you start ranking risks in the "Risk Ranking" section, this final score will determine where the risk falls in the list and whether it needs a response plan.

Quantitative Risk Analysis evaluates and quantifies risk exposure by assigning numeric values to the risk probabilities and impacts. The technique I discussed earlier, where you multiplied the probability value by the impact value to come up with an overall risk score, is a quantitative technique. However, that particular technique is closely related to qualitative techniques because it requires the use of the probability and impact scales to help determine an overall score.

Several other quantitative techniques exist, including sensitivity analysis, decision tree analysis, and simulation techniques. I'll discuss these techniques briefly in the following sections. Since most of these require extensive analysis and significant investments (in software and such), they aren't ideally suited to small-and-medium-sized projects.

Sensitivity Analysis

Sensitivity analysis is a modeling technique that determines which risk event (or events) has the greatest potential for impact. It's primarily concerned with risk events that impact time, cost, or anticipated project revenues (or cash flows) but can be used for any risk event.

You must establish a range of variation for each of these elements, including levels of acceptance. The effect of the risk event is assessed across this range. The higher the level of uncertainty about the risk, the more sensitive it is. And the most sensitive variables (usually those most critical to the project) are the ones that require risk response plans.

Decision Tree Analysis

Decision tree analysis is a diagramming method that shows the sequence of interrelated decisions and the expected results of choosing one alternative over another. It's usually used for risk events that impact time or cost.

You usually have more than one choice when faced with a risk event or a decision. Each possible decision is mapped in a tree form starting at the left, with the risk event and branches out to the right with possible outcomes. The following graphic shows a sample decision tree with the probability of two outcomes for the same risk event.

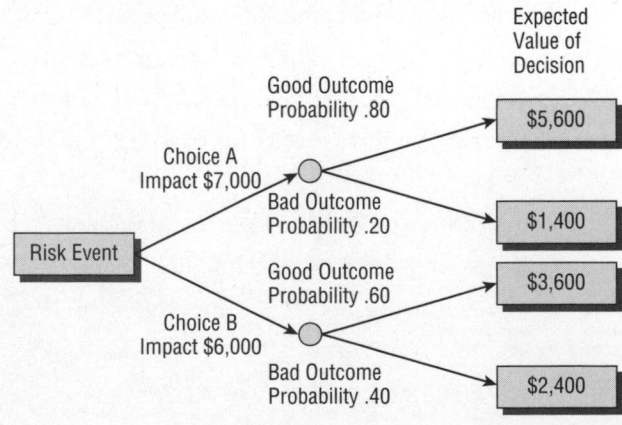

Choice A has a cost impact of $7,000, and Choice B has a cost impact of $6,000. If you were looking at those figures alone, you'd be tempted to choose Choice B. Depending on the objective you're trying to meet, you could interpret this analysis a couple of ways. If you want to maximize return while minimizing potential loss, you see that Choice A is the best decision because you stand to recoup more of your investment for a good outcome than you do for Choice B, and you'll lose less if the outcome is not so good. However, if your objective is solely to minimize loss, you'd choose Choice A because the probability of a bad outcome is less than the cost of the probability of a bad outcome for Choice B.

Simulation Techniques

Simulation techniques help you quantify risks associated with the project as a whole. *Monte Carlo analysis* is the most common simulation technique and requires the use of a computer and software written for this purpose.

Monte Carlo analysis typically examines schedule and cost risks both individually and from the perspective of the whole project. This analysis is performed by plugging in schedule and cost variables for each of the work packages from the work breakdown structure (WBS). Several variables may be used, including the pessimistic, most likely, and optimistic values or the mean and standard deviations. Monte Carlo then simulates potential outcomes of the project over and over using the range of variables. The outcome of this technique produces a reasonable range of schedule dates and costs for the project. It also shows you at a glance what the impact each of the variables has on the project as a whole.

The purpose of any risk analysis technique is to determine the impact the risk has on the project. It gives you a means to control the risk and determine if a response plan is needed instead of allowing risks to spark forest fires on their own during the project. It's most definitely worth your time and effort to perform this important step.

The Analysis Method of Choice

Qualitative Risk Analysis is the method of choice for small-to-medium-sized projects. Granted, there's some up-front investment of time needed to devise the scales, but it's a fairly easy thing to do—your team doesn't need to understand calculus and physics in order to develop or use the scales. Keep in mind that once you've gone through this effort, other teams can use these scales and you can reuse them on future projects. So it isn't a wasted effort by any means.

NOTE   The risk of not determining probability and impact of the project risk events has a high probability (80 percent by my scales) of biting your project in the backside.

Qualitative Risk Analysis is a simple method for determining risk values, and it provides a consistent way for the team to assess probability and impacts. And the more experienced the team members are with the organization, the types of projects the organization generally undertakes, and the risk tolerance levels, the more accurate your scales will be. This technique provides a level playing field for all project team members because the impacts relate to the organization's risk tolerance and everyone knows how significant *significant* is.

Listing and Ranking Project Risk

You've got your scores in hand. In the following sections I'll talk about what you do with them. Remember that your goal at the end of the risk analysis exercise (whether you use qualitative or quantitative techniques or a combination of both) is to rank the risks and determine which ones need further analysis and risk response plans. First let's look at ranking the risks.

As all good project managers—this includes you—know, there aren't many things you do in project management that you don't communicate and document. Before you put those rankings to use, let's document them.

Documenting Project Risk

During the identification process, you started a list of risks that includes an identification or tracking number, risk name, and risk description. The list could also include the category of risk for documentation purposes. I talked about this back in Chapter 2. You'll extend this list now to include the risk scores. Table 5.7 shows an example of how the risk list has grown. By the way, I'm using the five-point scale that ranges from High-High to Low-Low to determine scores.

TABLE 5.7: Example Risk List with Risk Scores

RISK ID	RISK	DESCRIPTION	PROBABILITY	IMPACT	RISK SCORE
1	Loss of key employee	Ned is an award-winning photojournalist who attracts nearly one third of your subscriber base. The magazine would suffer loss of subscribers if he left. Ned appears contented with his job and says he'll work here "until I die."	.05	.80	.04
2	Equipment breakdown or loss	Loss of Ned's favorite camera during the flight to Paris or malfunction of the equipment during the shoot could cause significant delays to the shoot and delays to production deadlines.	.40	.80	.32

You can see from glancing at this table that it's possible to not only identify the risks but also to assign their risk scores at the same time. Depending on the size and complexity of the project, you may have to get the risk team together only once to identify, rank order, and determine which risks need responses.

Risk Ranking

You'll now take the risk list one step further by prioritizing the risks into rank order. Since I've discussed a couple of ways to determine risk scores, you'll look at how to rank them under each scenario.

The first is the simple High-Medium-Low scale. I think this one is pretty easy to understand. All scores of High are assigned the highest ranking, Medium the next highest ranking, and so on. The idea is to rank the risks with the highest probability and highest impact first.

Now it gets tricky. You can also rank risks based on the probability and impact score separately, instead of a final score. For example, all High-High scores (high probability and high impact) are ranked higher than High-Medium scores, which are ranked higher than Low-Low scores.

I imagine you're seeing why I like calculating a final risk score, or expected value, using a scale that ranges from High-High to Low-Low. This means risks could be rated High-High probability and Medium impact, for example. That gets messy, so stick with a numeric score ($.80 \times .40 = .32$) for these values.

Calculating risk values like this makes ranking the risks a little easier. Otherwise, how do you know if the first risk with High-High is higher in priority than another risk with a High-High score? That may occasionally happen with a five-point value scale as well, but not as frequently. If you do have two risks with the same score, it will require a little more discussion among the group and weighing the impact of one risk over the other to determine how to rank them. An easy tiebreaker is to determine if one of the risks impacts a critical path task. If it does, and the other risk of the same score doesn't, rank the risk that impacts a critical path task higher than the other.

Now rank each of the risks according to their score. You can see that the risks with the highest impact and highest probability will be ranked first because their scores will be higher. Table 5.8 shows an example of a completed risk list.

TABLE 5.8: Rank-ordered Risk List

RANK	RISK ID	RISK	DESCRIPTION	PROBABILITY	IMPACT	RISK SCORE
1	2	Equipment breakdown or loss	Loss of Ned's favorite camera during the flight to Paris or malfunction of the equipment during the shoot could cause significant delays to the shoot and delays to production deadlines.	.40	.80	.32
2	1	Loss of key employee	Ned is an award-winning photojournalist who attracts nearly one third of your subscriber base. The magazine would suffer loss of subscribers if he left. Ned appears contented with his job and says he'll work here "until I die."	.05	.80	.04

This ranking will make the next step even easier.

Determining Risks That Need Response Plans

By the time you get to this step, it should be fairly smooth sailing. You've identified, analyzed, and ranked your risks from the highest combination of probability and impact to the lowest. It makes intuitive sense that the risks with the highest scores are the ones that will need response plans.

Use the same team of folks that helped you devise the risk scales to help determine the thresholds for requiring response plans. You can go about this in any number of ways. For example, let's say you're using the risk score as your method for ranking risks. You might devise a scale that looks something like this:

- Response plans required: Risk scores ≥ .15

- Response plans recommended: Risk scores >.02 and <.15

- Response plans not required: Risk scores ≤ .02

The recommended category may have an extra requirement stating that all risks that fall within this category must be reexamined at certain intervals of time.

You may also determine thresholds based on the probability and impact scores individually. In this case, the scale might look something like this:

- Any risk with a probability score ≥ .60 requires a response plan.

- Any risk with an impact score ≥ .40 requires a response plan.

If you're using the High-Medium-Low scale, response plans should probably be required for all Medium and High scores.

I think you're getting the hang of this. Again, it's a matter of understanding the project goals and the risk tolerance levels of the organization and project stakeholders, and reaching consensus with the risk team regarding scores and plan threshold values.

Case Study

Emily Lewis has put together a risk team composed of two key stakeholders and three project team members to perform risk analysis. She interviewed the project sponsor, Bill Olsen, regarding risk tolerance levels of the organization and his own risk tolerance levels. She brought that information with her to some brainstorming sessions she conducted with the risk management team to analyze the risks and assign probability and impacts.

The team members first determined they'd use the following scale for both probability and impact ratings:

High-High: .80

High: .60

Medium: .40

Low: .20

Low-Low: .05

The team examined their risk list from Chapter 2 and came up with the risk scores shown in Table 5.9. (For the sake of space, the Category and Owner columns have been eliminated from this table.)

TABLE 5.9: Risk Scores

ID	RISK	DESCRIPTION	PROBABILITY	IMPACT	RISK SCORE
1	Interface	The CRM system doesn't interface with the ERP system.	.05	.80	.04
2	Transfer of data	Accurate transfer of knowledge tree data from existing CRM to new CRM.	.60	.40	.24
3	Transfer of customer data	Accurate transfer of customer account information from existing CRM to new CRM.	.05	.80	.04
4	Equipment	More equipment will be needed than identified in the project proposal.	.40	.40	.16
5	Key personnel	Subject matter expert on the existing CRM system leaves prior to design of the new system.	.60	.60	.24
6	Project management	Project management processes aren't fully established.	.20	.20	.04
7	Space	No space for additional servers and equipment.	.60	.20	.12
8	Posting of data	Posting of data to existing and new customer accounts.	.20	.80	.16

The team members also documented the assumptions they made regarding these risks and their probability and impact. Here are the assumptions for the first two risk events:

Interface The assumptions are that the new CRM system is a well-documented system with many installations across the country. It has been proven that the CRM system will work with your existing ERP system in other installations. If it didn't interface with the ERP system for some reason, the impact would cause severe delays to the project schedule and potentially jeopardize the completion of the project.

Transfer of data Your organization's knowledge data is a homegrown application. Although you think it's possible to convert this data and import it to the new system, you've never done anything like this. The vendor assures you it has examined the data and the transfer should be no problem. If there are problems, it won't prevent the system from being implemented (or affect your go-live date), but the customer service reps will be impacted, as they'll have to refer to paper manuals until the knowledge tree is populated.

The risk team determined that all risks with a score greater than or equal to .16 need a response plan. Therefore, the following risks require risk response plans:

- Transfer of data
- Equipment
- Key personnel
- Posting of data

CHAPTER 6

Defining Risk Response Plans

You've identified your risks, analyzed them for their impacts on the project, assigned probabilities and impact values, determined an expected value, and ranked them in order. You've also determined which of the risks, given all those conditions, require response plans. This chapter discusses what risk response plans are, the techniques for developing response plans, and how to document and write plans for those risks that have a high probability and high impact on the project. Let's get to it.

Risk Response Planning

Risk Response Planning is the process of deciding what actions to take to reduce threats (especially to schedule and cost) while taking advantage of the opportunities other risks present.

Typically, you'll want to develop risk response plans for risks with the potential for high probability and high impact. It isn't efficient to spend time writing response plans for risks you've determined aren't likely to occur and won't impact the project significantly if they do. For example, if I'm building a tourist center in the Mojave Desert, I wouldn't spend time on a risk response plan for the possibility of rain. It does rain in the Mojave (an average of 2.5 inches per year), so the possibility exists, but it's highly unlikely it would impact my project. I'll deal with these types of risks in the "Contingency Planning" section a little later in this chapter.

NOTE Developing well-written, detailed risk response plans will increase your chances for a successful project and decrease your overall project risk.

Remember that risk management planning, including the development of risk response plans, isn't a one-time exercise. As you progress through the project and learn more about potential risk events, you'll reevaluate their impacts, which may require a change in strategy to deal with the risk and a new or revised response plan. And even though I've focused primarily on risks that prevent you from meeting the goals of the project, don't forget that risks can produce opportunities.

Uncertain Certainty

One thing is certain: your project does have risks, and if you choose to ignore them, your project will have an uncertain outcome. All project risk is closely linked with the availability of information and communication, or the lack thereof, as I've talked about previously. The more information you have, the more likely you're able to predict the risk event and its impacts. And the better you're able to predict risk impacts, the better you'll be at creating risk response plans.

When thinking about risk response plans, keep in mind that risk outcomes generally fall into three categories:

- Known risks with predictable outcomes
- Known risks with uncertain outcomes
- Unknown risks with unpredictable outcomes

These are fairly straightforward. A *known risk* is something you know has the potential to happen. The term *predictable outcomes* implies you know with reasonable certainty what the impacts and outcomes of the risk events would be if they occurred. *Unpredictable outcomes* are impacts and consequences of the risk event that aren't fully identified or known.

Let's use a simple example to explain each of these outcomes. You've decided to paint your garage door this weekend. One risk that could keep you from completing this project is the weather. No problem—you cruise the Internet and check out the local forecast, which predicts clear and sunny skies, with little possibility of showers. You have the means to learn about the weather (the Internet site) and to determine the certainty of the impact (a 10 percent chance of showers). That means you know, with predictable certainty, that this risk has a low chance of occurring.

Known risks with uncertain outcomes are more difficult because, well, their outcomes aren't certain. However, the amount of uncertainty could vary. You may, for example, know it's going to rain but not know when it'll start or how long it'll continue. When you're facing project risks with uncertain outcomes, I recommend learning everything you can about the risk and its possible impacts. (Since the impacts are unpredictable, this isn't always possible.) You should interview stakeholders, research past projects, and try to move as far from the uncertainty end of the spectrum as you can. The more you know, the better.

The last bullet listed previously, unknown risks with unpredictable outcomes, says you don't know about the risk and you don't know about its impacts. It's an unknown risk with an unknown outcome. Suppose you're happily painting away and are three-quarters finished when a flock of geese happens to fly right over your house. You guessed it. An unknown risk with an unpredictable outcome has occurred.

NOTE   Unknown risks with unpredictable outcomes, by their definition, can't be identified ahead of time. If you have an uncanny ability to see into the future, you could identify these risks and their impacts. But then they'd be known risks instead of unknown risks.

Many project decisions are made without benefit of knowing all the facts, and risk analysis is no exception. Risk, after all, is primarily about uncertainty. Analyzing the risks tells you about the possible outcomes for the risk, and the response plan addresses how to deal with those outcomes. The greater your certainty of the outcome, the easier it will be to develop response plans. For example, if you know rain is a certainty on the day you're planning on painting the garage, you can devise response plans that are fairly precise. You could postpone the painting to another day and sweep the garage floor instead.

Or, perhaps you know with reasonable certainty that the rain is coming but won't start until early afternoon. In that case, you could quickly paint the door in the morning while the sun is still out (or the clouds are rolling in) and then flip open the door so it's protected by the garage ceiling until it dries.

Purpose of Planning for Risks

The purpose for risk planning is to determine the most appropriate response to reduce, control, or take advantage of the risk event. Along with determining the response, you'll want to make certain you're choosing the right strategy for the risk event. After determining the strategy to use, you'll develop an action plan to put this strategy into play should the risk event occur.

The second purpose for risk planning is to determine a risk owner. I talked about risk owners and their responsibility in Chapter 2, "Identifying and Documenting Risks." Once the plan is developed, the risk owner is the one held accountable for watching for risk triggers, tracking the risk, recommending the implementation of the response plan if the situation warrants it, and then monitoring the effectiveness of the response plan once it's implemented.

Risk response planning also has an added benefit. When risk events do occur, you'll be able to remain calm, cool, and levelheaded about what to do. Rather than reacting like our friend Ned, you'll calmly reach for the response plan document and know what to do. When you're in panic mode, the object is to resolve the problem as quickly as possible. That means you usually deal with things the quickest and easiest way you can think of just to get everything under control. But getting immediate control doesn't necessarily solve the problem in the long run. Response planning allows you determine the best method for dealing with a risk, which gives you a higher probability of meeting your project goals.

MONSTERS

Two very special girls I know love the children's book titled *The Monster at the End of This Book* by Jon Stone and Michael Smollin. The premise of the book is Grover, the main character, tries everything he can to prevent getting to the end of the book because he doesn't want to confront the monster that lives there.

The younger of the two girls will ask me to read the book over and over again and tremble in my lap as I'm reading. She is petrified we're going to find a monster at the end of the book even though she knows the ending and can recite the story almost word for word.

Risk response planning provides a way to deal with the monster and his threats *before* you get to the end of the project. Without response plans, you're in reactive—rather than proactive—mode, and you may very well find a monster at the end of the project. If you take the time to develop risk response plans, you'll usually find the monster was nothing much at all because the plan took care of the monster's threat.

I can assure you that the ending to the children's book is much friendlier than the ending to your projects will be without having adequate risk response plans in place.

Risk Response Techniques

You have several strategies for dealing with risk that help reduce or control the impacts of risk events. The most common strategies are as follows:

- Avoidance
- Transference

- Mitigation
- Acceptance
- Contingency planning
- Independent verification and validation

Each of these techniques has its strengths and weaknesses. Before determining which strategy to use, make certain you understand the type of risk you're dealing with, as well as the severity of the risk. You'll want to choose the strategy that will be the most effective and cost efficient for dealing with the risk event. If it costs you more to respond to the risk than the consequences of the risk itself, you may want to consider a different strategy.

Avoidance

You may have already guessed that the risk *avoidance* technique is about avoiding risk. True. It encompasses more than that, however. Risk avoidance techniques include the following:

- Avoiding the risk altogether
- Eliminating the cause of the risk event
- Changing the project plan to protect the objectives from the risk event

Let's look at some examples for each technique. Avoiding the risk altogether implies that you know the outcomes of the risk with relative certainty and can take steps to keep the risk event from occurring. Suppose Ned and the photo-shoot team are headed to the airport to catch their flight to Paris. In keeping with Ned's usual manner, he has held everyone up to the last second. If they leave any later, they won't have time to check the million pieces of luggage Ned is bringing and get through security in time to catch the flight. Sherry, the quick-thinking project manager, decides to do a traffic check before leaving. She logs onto the Internet and finds there's been a major accident on the highway they were planning on taking to the airport. To avoid delays and keep them from missing the flight,

Sherry decides on an alternate route that bypasses the accident and avoids the risk event.

Eliminating the cause of the risk is a technique that works something like this. Sherry knows that the team's luggage looks like every other piece of luggage they're likely to see on an airport conveyor belt. The team is carrying some sensitive company information and a few pieces of specialized equipment. Sherry can eliminate the cause of this risk by carrying the company material and specialized equipment on board in their carry-ons.

One of the objectives of the photo assignment is to shoot pictures of Parisians doing everyday tasks—strolling through the park, eating at sidewalk cafés, shopping, and so on—outside in the open air. A rainstorm pops up on the day this shoot is supposed to occur. Sherry changes the project plan by switching an indoor shooting day with the outdoor shooting day to protect the project objectives from the risk event.

NOTE Avoidance is the technique of choice when it comes to scope and schedule creep risk. How do you avoid these risks? You avoid them by gathering requirements and breaking them into their smallest components, documenting project scope, obtaining quality estimates, preparing a schedule that accurately reflects the work of the project, and monitoring the project for adherence to the plan.

Avoidance is a great strategy when you can use it. The trouble is it isn't appropriate for every risk, so let's look at some more techniques.

Transference

Transference is a technique that transfers the risk and its consequences to a third party. The risk hasn't gone away, but the responsibility for managing that risk now rests with someone else. Transference techniques include the following:

- Insurance
- Contracting

- Warranties
- Guarantees
- Performance bonds

The transference technique is most effective when dealing with financial risks, as you can tell by the types of techniques included in this category. You're all familiar with insurance. Suppose you catch strep throat. You have to go to the doctor's office, get a test, and then get a prescription to get rid of the vicious bug. If you have health insurance, chances are you didn't have to pay the full cost for the visit or the tests. The insurance company pays the majority of the expenses. However, there's a cost to you. You pay monthly premiums for the benefit of the insurance company bearing the risk of medical expenses. So, you transfer the risk of possible medical expenses to the insurance company and pay a premium to do so.

Contracting is a form of transferring specific risks to the vendor per the terms of the contract. The vendor accepts the responsibility for the cost of failure. This doesn't come without a price either. Contractors charge for the services, and depending on the type of contract you negotiate, the cost can be high.

NOTE   Contracting isn't a cure-all. And you may be swapping one risk for another. If the vendor can't fulfill the obligations per the contract, your project can suffer serious delays or termination.

Warranties, guarantees, and performance bonds work much the same way in that the risk of failure is transferred to another party.

Most of these techniques come with a price, so you'll need to account for their costs in your project budget.

Mitigation

Risk *mitigation* attempts to reduce the probability of a risk event and its impacts to an acceptable level. This is the most common strategy in risk response planning. Let's revisit Ned and Sherry for this one.

As stated earlier, Ned and Sherry's luggage contains some sensitive company information. Sherry knows their luggage looks like every other piece of luggage coming down an airport conveyor belt. To mitigate the risk of someone else accidentally picking up a team member's bags, Sherry ties brightly colored braided cords on the handles of each bag and attaches laminated business cards to each of the cords.

Mitigation planning can introduce new risks to the project if you're not watching. For example, tying ribbons to the luggage may cause it to get caught in equipment, which could hold up the delivery of the luggage.

Acceptance

Acceptance means you won't make any plans to avoid or mitigate the risk. You're willing to accept the consequences of the risk event should it occur. Acceptance may also happen by default because the risk team was unable to come up with an acceptable response strategy for a risk.

Contingency Planning

Contingency planning involves planning alternatives to deal with the risks should they occur. This technique is a form of acceptance because if the risk event occurs, you're willing to accept the consequences, but you take it one step further and devise a plan to deal with the consequences.

This is different from mitigation and the other techniques because mitigation attempts to reduce the probability and the impact of the risk event. Contingency planning recognizes the risk is likely to occur, and while it requires a plan, contingency planning doesn't attempt to reduce the impact of the risk; it's simply a plan to deal with its consequences.

Sherry from the photo-shoot project used a contingency plan to deal with Ned losing his passport. She copied the front page of Ned's passport prior to leaving the office. When they got to the airport, she was able to contact the American Embassy and get Ned a new passport. (Yes, I know what you're thinking...Ned had to use his passport to get on the plane in the first place, so where could it be? What can I say? Ned is not well organized and lost it somewhere between the time he boarded the plane and landed in Paris. Knowing Ned, it could be anywhere.) This didn't eliminate or reduce the probability for the risk occurring, but a clear plan was in place to deal with the event when and if it happened.

Contingency planning is the technique to use for unknown risks with unknown outcomes. I'll talk more about that in the "Contingency Planning" section of this chapter.

THE BUTTERFLY WING

The local zoo is planning a project to add a butterfly wing to the tropical house. The project is greatly anticipated by zoo staff and citizens. The zoo does a fantastic job of advertising and generating interest in the new wing—too good, in fact. On opening day, the turnout is much greater than projected, and the zoo has to turn people away.

Fortunately, the project manager developed a contingency plan for this risk event by printing reduced-admission coupons. The zoo gave coupons to everyone it had to turn away on opening day so they could visit on another day at a discounted price.

Some of the risks I've talked about regarding Ned's project could be handled more than one way. The loss of equipment risk is a good example. The project manager could eliminate the cause of the risk by dividing the equipment (mitigation), she could have shipped it all ahead of time via a carrier and insured each piece in case of loss (avoidance and transference), or she could have located a camera supplier in Paris who carries Ned's favorite equipment and replaced any lost equipment (contingency). Table 6.1 lists the risks I've talked about in this chapter and some possible strategies for dealing with them. (There are more strategies for some of these than what's listed.)

TABLE 6.1: Risk Events and Possible Strategies

RISK EVENT	POSSIBLE STRATEGIES
Missing the flight because of traffic jams	Avoidance: Check traffic before leaving, and take an alternate route.
	Contingency: Plan an alternate route in case of traffic jam.
	Mitigation: Spend the night before the flight in an airport hotel.
Luggage taken from baggage claim	Avoidance: Carry company information on board.
	Transference: Insure bags for loss.
	Mitigation: Tie braided ribbons to bags.
Unable to take photos of Parisians outdoors	Avoidance: Change the project plan.
	Contingency: Take pictures of Parisians indoors, and edit them into stock pictures of Paris.
Losing equipment	Mitigation: Divide equipment into several cases.
	Transference: Overnight the equipment prior to leaving, and insure each package.
	Contingency: Purchase lost equipment in Paris.
Losing passport	Avoidance: Leave Ned home.
	Contingency: Take copy of passports for easier replacement from the embassy.

Each of these strategies and their accompanying responses has its advantages, and each carries a cost. You'll look at weighing the costs of these strategies in the "Risk Response Costs" section later in this chapter.

IV&V

Another strategy that's useful involves hiring contractors to perform *independent verification and validation (IV&V)* of the project and the project management processes. This strategy is used more often for large projects and usually for those that are outsourced. However, if you're working on a project that's more complex than anything you've undertaken in the past, you may want to consider this approach.

The idea with IV&V is that a third-party vendor is hired to oversee the project. They attend all status meetings, review documents, review deliverables, review the project management processes, and so on. They rate the project according to predefined objectives. You almost always want IV&V looking out for the schedule. The reason this is a useful and successful technique is because you have a third set of eyes looking at every aspect of the project. They can alert the project manager to risks or potential problems on the project that no one else has seen. They will also give you an honest assessment of how the vendor that's performing the work of the project itself is doing and where improvement is needed. I don't envy the folks who fill this role. It's a tough job because they're always in the middle. They're hired to be objective and report the truth, and sometimes that means they have to bite the hand that feeds them. But I'd much rather have someone watch the project for risks with me. They can warn me about them while there's still time to do something. It's better than being blindsided and having no plans in place to deal with the risk.

TIP　It's usually easier to take action early on that will reduce the probability and impact of a risk than it is to fix the damage once it's done.

Developing Risk Response Plans

Risk Response Plans are usually developed around one or more of the strategies I talked about in the previous section. The type and severity of the risk determine the level of risk response planning that should be done. Well-documented and well-written response plans are your primary defense to reduce risk impacts and control as much about the risk event as possible. Of course, you can take advantage of any opportunities that present themselves as well.

Risk response plans should include at least the following information:

- Risk ID number
- Risk name and description (including the risk's effect on the project scope)
- Risk originator
- Risk owner
- Probability
- Impact
- Expected value (risk score)
- Any information needed to track and monitor the risk throughout the project
- Risk triggers
- Response plan
- Resources needed to implement the plan

NOTE You can find a Risk Response Plan template on the Sybex website at www.sybex.com.

Let's work through an example. Suppose you've identified a risk that concerns lack of sponsor involvement. The impacts of this risk are delayed responses to escalated questions and problems that could cause schedule delays. The risk triggers, response plans, and resources may look like the following.

Risk triggers Sponsor stops attending project status meetings. Sponsor doesn't respond in a timely manner to questions and issues. Sponsor is often unavailable.

Risk response Mitigation: Meet with sponsor to discuss importance of sponsor's availability. Set up recurring weekly meetings with sponsor to go over project issues. Contingency: Identify another key stakeholder who can make project decisions or influence the sponsor appropriately.

Resources needed Project manager's time, sponsor's time.

You'll recall that risk triggers are symptoms that a risk event is about to occur. When you develop your response plans, be certain to include the risk triggers as well. You'll want to review risk triggers and the response plans when the risk event presents itself. In this example, several triggers may indicate the risk is imminent. When two of these triggers present within a short amount of time, it's an even stronger indication the risk event is coming. You can also use what you've learned about the trigger and the risk response later in the process when performing risk audits.

Calling All Resources

Response plans require resources to implement no matter how you slice it. You may need to buy materials, hire contractors, purchase insurance, or perform any number of other tasks to implement the plan. Even if no material resources are needed, human resources will always be required.

Human resources are never "free." I hear many project managers make that mistake. For example, they save money by not purchasing training with a new installation of software because they have a crack team that doesn't need training. "They can pick it up on their own." That's all well and good, but while those resources are busy "picking it up on their own," they aren't completing project tasks (or other functional tasks). If these same resources are resources assigned to your project, you've just introduced new risk and potentially created schedule creep.

Resources, no matter what they're doing, cost the company money. Their salaries aren't free, and neither are the benefits the company provides. So, make the most of your resources by making wise project decisions and investments.

Risk Response Costs

As I mentioned earlier, you should consider the financial cost of implementing each response. If the response plan costs more than the consequences of the risk event, ditch the plan and accept the risk. The same idea applies to the time and effort it takes to develop the response plan. If the response plan is so complex that it requires more time and effort than it would take the team to deal with consequences of the risk event itself, accept the risk.

Table 6.1 showed some of the strategies Ned's project manager might choose for the risk events. Let's compare the costs of the consequences of the risk event with the cost of responses.

Missing the flight because of traffic jams

Impact of the risk event occurring: $600 (the cost of changing four international tickets to a different time).

Cost of avoidance: a few minutes of time to check the traffic route before leaving.

Cost of contingency: an extra 15 minutes of commute time to take an alternate route.

Cost of mitigation: $1,000 for the team to stay in the hotel the night before the flight.

Conclusion: avoidance or contingency plans should be considered. Mitigation costs more than the consequence of the risk event.

Loss of equipment

Impact of the risk event occurring: $25,000.

Cost of mitigation: $750 to purchase cases.

Transference: $350 to overnight everything and insure it in case of loss.

Contingency: $28,000 to purchase lost equipment in Paris, plus the time and effort required to buy it.

You can see the logic being used to determine one response over another. Keep in mind that cost won't always be the deciding factor. Sometimes, depending on the project and the impacts, you have to implement the plan regardless of the cost of the response.

Documenting the Response Plans

I've talked about documenting quite often throughout this book. I hope I don't have to do much convincing of the importance of documenting your response plans.

Response plans should be accessible by all project team members and stakeholders. The risk owners need access to the plans in order to monitor them and recommend implementation of the plans. Stakeholders may also want to review the plans—particularly if the risk event or its response plan impacts their business areas. Publish the location of the documents with your project status report so everyone knows where they can find the information.

You may also want to consider adding the risk response information to the risk database I talked about in Chapter 2. You probably wouldn't document the entire response plan there, but a brief listing or explanation of the strategies identified for the plan would be appropriate.

Planning for the Unknown

Uncertainty is a lack of knowledge. Obviously, unknown risks with unknown outcomes are risks that don't exist on your risk identification list because you don't know about them.

NOTE Uncertainty is inherent in project management. That's why communication and documentation are your best friends throughout the life of the project. Make certain you're in constant communication with the project team, the stakeholders, the vendors, and any other interested parties. The more you know, the less uncertainty there is.

By its nature, uncertainty occurs mostly outside the project, but not always. Elements such as the economy, social issues, environmental issues, financial stability of the organization, the management team, other projects, and so on, can cause uncertainty and unknown risks to occur on your project.

I'm not letting you off the hook quite that easily, though. Not all surprises can be classified as unpredictable risks with unknown outcomes. Some are really predictable risks with unknown outcomes because the risk could (and should) have been identified during the risk identification process but was simply missed. Nonetheless, contingencies come to the rescue.

I talked about contingency plans a little earlier in this chapter. Contingencies are a form of acceptance and don't attempt to reduce the probability or impact of the risk. Risks that your team didn't plan on do and will occur, and contingencies are how you deal with them. I'll cover some of the reasons for developing contingency plans next and then follow that with a discussion of contingency reserves.

Things That Go Bump

Typically, the things that go wrong on a project have to do with one or more of these three elements (or a combination of any of the three):

- Project schedule
- Project performance
- Costs

These elements are the reasons why you develop time and cost contingency reserves for the project. The next section will cover time and cost reserves more fully. First, though, let's take a look at some of the causes of each of these problems.

Schedule issues, of course, impact whether the project is completed on time. Some causes of schedule uncertainties are the following:

- Poor estimates
- Resource availability
- Materials availability
- Late deliveries

- Uncontrolled or excessive scope and schedule changes
- Lack of timely decisions

Project performance has to do with performing the work of the project while satisfying the goals of the project. A host of problems can cause performance issues, including but not limited to the following:

- Team morale
- Politics
- Lack of timely decisions
- Changes in technology
- Poor quality
- Slow production times
- Project team changes
- Loss of project sponsor
- Management changes
- Inadequate project management processes
- Unreliable and unsecure technology

Performance issues may fall in either the time or the cost camp, or both, depending on the project and the issue. For example, management changes may impact the schedule because decisions have to be delayed until the new team is in place, or they may impact cost because new managers may divert funds from your project to others (or contribute more funds to your project). Again, you'll have to examine these causes and impacts to determine if a response plan is needed or if a contingency plan will work.

Costs may fluctuate for a host of reasons as well. Some of them include the following:

- Schedule delays
- Inadequate procurement processes
- Poor estimates

- Market demand
- Technology
- Resource availability

Get consensus from your risk team after examining the risk impacts against the project objectives and their complexities. Look at the reasons for the risk and its impact to determine if a response plan is needed or if a contingency will suffice.

Contingency Reserves

In addition to contingency plans, typically you can develop two types of contingency reserves for the project. They are time and cost contingencies.

Contingency reserves are the amount of time or money set aside to deal with risks. How much should you set aside? Unfortunately, there isn't a magic formula for calculating contingency reserves. I wish I could tell you, "Add 25 percent to your schedule and 15 percent to your budget for contingency reserves," but I can't.

That means your risk team has another task. They should determine the appropriate amount of contingency reserves for the risks that don't need response plans. These reserves (or *buffers*, as some folks call them) should take the following into consideration:

- Risk tolerance levels of management and stakeholders
- Adequacy and thoroughness of the risk management processes (identification, analysis, and prioritization)
- Overall levels of risk associated with the project (is there a significant number of high probability/high impact risks?)
- Complexity of the project
- Experience levels of the project team with similar projects
- Historical information for projects of similar size and scope

Basic cost contingencies take into account the variableness in the cost of resources. If your project has a short timeline, cost variances aren't likely to occur. However, the longer the time frame, the greater the potential for variances. Sometimes this can work in your favor. Computer equipment manufacturers, for example, continually improve functionality and features. You may have budgeted $5,000 for a server with a particular configuration and find when you go to purchase it that it actually has more capability than what you originally planned.

Basic contingencies are a good idea if you're purchasing a lot of goods or materials. We've all experienced purchasing items at the store today at one price only to find next week the very same item has gone up in price.

Don't be afraid to spend your contingencies. Some project managers build in contingencies and vow never to touch them. If you're using this ploy to increase your bonus at the end of the project—hmmm, you've got some 'splaining to do.

NOTE   Ensure the safety of your project—implement contingency reserves, and don't be afraid to spend the money when needed.

Time contingencies should be examined and determined the same way as cost buffers. Previous experience working with the team or vendors will tell you if they tend to overestimate or underestimate tasks. You can also look at past projects that are similar in scope and complexity to see the amount of reserves that were set. Don't go overboard when figuring time buffers if you're confident your estimates are accurate and your team is experienced at estimating tasks of this nature.

Whether or not you use contingencies, you should examine every risk for the best possible response plan. Don't rely excessively on contingencies, or you could end up with so many of them that you put the project in danger. Contingencies are more appropriate for risks with minimal probability and impact.

Buffering Stakeholders

One of the dangers of adding contingency reserves to your schedule and budget is having stakeholders accuse you of creating a buffer—which is exactly what you're doing—only they don't mean it as a compliment!

This is an education and communication process. Contingencies aren't a means to make yourself look good. They're a legitimate project management technique to account for unplanned risks on the project. If possible, spend some time educating your stakeholders on the purpose of contingencies so they know what you're doing and why you're doing it. The point is to reduce the impacts of risks on the project. The stakeholders want a successful project on time and on budget, right? Contingency reserves will help make that happen.

If all else fails and you happen to work for nasty stakeholders (hey, it happens), inform your sponsor about the contingencies but don't broadcast the news to the stakeholders. I'm not telling you to lie—if they ask, tell them. But this is one of only a few instances I can think of that not telling them may be to your benefit.

Case Study

Emily's team is working on the inventory piece of the new CRM system. The credit-card-scanning machines progress through five stations, the final of which is the packaging stage. The fourth station, finishing, is where the inventory information is captured by the CRM system. During testing, a problem occurred in finishing that wasn't anticipated during the risk response planning stage. The inventory information isn't uploading to the CRM system. Since the machines won't progress to the final stage without first having been inventoried, all the machines in test are piling up at the finishing stage. This means no machines are getting shipped to customers—not good.

Fortunately for Emily and the team, they have contingencies in place. The team did anticipate there may be unknown problems in the testing phase and devised a plan to deal with those unknowns.

The contingency plan includes identifying and documenting the problem. Next, a team member is assigned as the owner of the problem. The vendor is also alerted to the problem, and if they're involved, they assign a team member to the problem as well. The person (or team) who is performing the work of this deliverable is brought in on the issue, and together with Emily, the risk owner, and other stakeholders if necessary, they come up with a detailed plan that addresses this specific problem including tasks, estimated time frames, and costs. If the time or cost consumes more than the contingency reserves, Emily will brief the project sponsor and determine if a change request is in order to accommodate the changes to scope, schedule, or cost.

Additionally, new risks have been identified since the risk list was developed, and they've been added to the list. The following is an example of a risk response plan for the new risk, subcontractor failure:

Risk ID number: 9 **Risk:** Subcontractor failure

Risk originator: Emily Lewis **Risk owner:** Maria, Procurement

Probability: .60 **Impact:** .80

Expected value: .48

Description: The vendor who is programming and installing the CRM system has subcontracted programming services to help stay on schedule.

Impact: Not completing the programming on time will cause schedule delays. A positive impact of this risk is programmers with slack time in their schedules can assist in other programming activities, such as testing and resolving bugs and problems.

Additional information: Test scripts should accurately reflect the appropriate steps in the process. Business user experts should review and execute test scripts.

Risk triggers: Extension of task dates, revision of estimates, missed deliverable dates.

Response plan: Require the primary vendor to secure a performance bond in case of failure. Require the primary vendor to maintain an active list of available subcontractors for substitution of current subcontractor if necessary.

Resources needed to implement plan: Procurement, IT experts to review status of programming.

CHAPTER 7

Implementing and Monitoring Risk Response Plans

You've reached the last two steps in the risk management processes: monitoring risk response plans and performing risk audits. In this chapter, I'll discuss how and when to implement risk plans, the ongoing importance of monitoring the project for risks, and the benefits of performing risk audits.

Monitoring and Control

Risk Monitoring and Control is concerned with monitoring the status of risks associated with the project, monitoring the project environment, and responding to risks as they occur. The risk management plan (I talked about this in Chapter 1, "What Is Risk Management?") details how risk is managed overall, and the risk response plan details how the risk response strategies are implemented. Risk monitoring and control is about putting the plans into action and examining the results of those plans. This involves the following:

- Tracking and monitoring identified risks

- Responding to risks as they occur

- Monitoring residual and secondary risks

- Identifying new risks

- Evaluating risk response plans that are put into action

- Monitoring for risk triggers

- Ensuring that risk policies and procedures are followed

- Ensuring that risk response plans and contingency plans are appropriate and effective

One of the most important activities of this stage is, oddly enough, monitoring. *Monitoring* is an activity that includes gathering information, documenting the findings, and then reporting them. Some of the information you should review includes the previous list. In addition, you'll want to monitor the project environment. By this I mean what's happening in and around the project that may impact the project or change or impact the risk responses. When thinking about the project environment, consider these issues:

- Customers
- Technology
- Management team
- Project sponsor status
- Social impacts
- Industry trends
- Economics
- Legal issues
- Financial issues
- Safety issues
- Politics

Uncertainty (which is what risk events are) often occurs outside the bounds of the project. Most of the items on the previous project environment list are factors outside the project. Suppose the economy is headed into a recession. This could impact your project in several ways. Availability of funds may become an issue. Customers may change their orders or scope of work because of their own constraints pertaining to the economic situation. Market demand for the product may decrease or increase, availability of materials could be impacted, and so on. Any of these issues can cause new risks to the project or impact response plans that you've previously developed.

NOTE   Monitoring the project environment is as important as monitoring the project itself.

From within the bounds of the project you'll want to examine the project status, review risks lists and assumptions, watch for risk triggers, review change requests, and review response plans prior to implementing. After implementing, you'll want to monitor the plans and put corrective actions into place for those plans that aren't effective and develop contingency plans. Let's look at each of these areas next.

Project Temperature

Project status meetings are perfect opportunities for you to examine risk identification lists, listen to what team members are telling you (both verbally and nonverbally), and examine response plans that have been put into action. Risk owners are the ones responsible for monitoring risks, so set aside time at each meeting for the risk owners to report their risk status.

The following are some of the areas you'll want to pay particular attention to during status meetings:

- Scope
- Schedule
- Resources
- Quality

I've covered these issues in depth previously, but for those of you who've skipped ahead to this chapter, I'll provide a high-level review.

You examine scope to determine if the work of the project is on track with the goals of the project. If the work of the project starts drifting off track from the goals, you're in danger of project risk. And scope changes will cause schedule changes, so now you have a double whammy.

Schedule issues can involve untimely delays (materials, vendors, resources, services), team member absences, scope creep, and so on.

Resources may not be available when promised, skills and experience may not be adequate for tasks at hand, employees may have poor morale, and lack of motivation may also cause project risks.

Quality issues concern meeting testing criteria, performance measures, customer satisfaction, and so on.

Risk Review

You'll have to reach back to Chapter 1 and remember a couple of things you've learned so far. The probability of risks occurring is higher during the Initiating and Planning processes than later in the project. However, the impacts of risk events are lower in these phases and increase as the project progresses. As you review the risk list, keep in mind that depending on the life-cycle phase the project is in, more or fewer of these risks may occur. You'll see lots of activity early on but much bigger impacts as the project progresses.

Let's say you're in the early stages of the Planning process. You've identified the loss of a key employee as a risk and documented the assumptions concerning this risk. The score for this risk fell below your threshold for a response plan, so one was never developed. However, being the great project manager that you are, you set aside time at every status meeting to review the risk list.

Fast forward to the Executing phase. So far, so good—the risk event hasn't occurred. However, you've learned from a credible source that a key employee has been in contact with a competitor of yours. Knowing what you know about this employee's work and reputation, you know any competitor would snap him up in a minute. At this point, it's time to reexamine your assumptions. Originally, you assumed this employee was content at his job. Now you have evidence to the contrary. It's time to reexamine this risk, reexamine its assumptions, and determine if a response plan is needed.

You should review assumptions about the risks as you review the risk list because assumptions will change. For example, today you may assume materials are available on a moment's notice from your favorite supplier. Tomorrow, however, that supplier could sell out to a larger company. Therefore, your assumptions must change based on the change in ownership, and those assumptions may dictate changes to the response plan.

Risk Triggers

Risk triggers warn of impending risk events. If you've devised your risk list so that it includes a column for triggers, it's a simple matter to review the triggers along with the risk list.

You want your team members engaged in this review activity. If you all silently glance down the list during the status meeting and nod your heads, you're not accomplishing much. Worse yet, risk events will sneak up from behind and catch you off guard. Put your risk owners and your team members on the spot. Ask them pointed questions about their tasks and their progress. Ask them if they know of anything brewing that should be reported. Ask them about triggers, conversations with suppliers and vendors, and how implemented response plans are performing.

Change Requests

Change requests may bring about their own risks. Part of the change management procedure should include reviewing change requests for the introduction of new risks.

Project priorities may also change. When that happens, ordinarily there are changes to scope, schedule, or budget as a result. Depending on the complexity of these changes, the project plan may need to be reworked, which means the risk management processes should be repeated. Don't rely on old assumptions or previously identified risk lists when significant changes have occurred to the project. They're good starting places, but don't fool yourself into thinking you've already got the risks and risk response plans in place so there's no need to repeat them.

Correcting Plans

The control part of the Risk Monitoring and Control equation involves taking action to prevent or mitigate risk, which may also include correcting the response plans. Remember that most response plans were written prior to the work of the project starting. At that point, assumptions were made and risk scores assigned and evaluated to determine if a plan should be developed. Now a risk event is upon you. Let's suppose Ned and Sherry, our photojournalist friends, are discussing the day's events at a local bistro. Ned has discovered a love for French wine and maybe is a little overzealous with his affection today. He snatches Sherry to her feet and thrusts them both into a dance pose. He takes a few steps and sends Sherry into an unexpected twirl. She loses her balance and reaches out for the table to steady herself. She was traveling a bit faster than she anticipated, and her hand sails across the top of the table, sending both of Ned's favorite camera lenses crashing to the ground.

Sherry assures Ned there's no problem since she arranged with Ned's favorite camera supplier to overnight anything they need. According to the risk response plan, Sherry calls their contact and asks them to ship the two lenses. Problem: the lens Ned uses most often is out of stock. Wait—that scenario wasn't part of the plan. This means Ned and Sherry will have to correct and adapt the response plan to deal with the risk. Want to know how Sherry corrects the plan and mitigates the risk? You'll have to read my next book…just kidding. Fortunately, Sherry researched photography stores prior to leaving the United States and created a list with phone numbers and addresses. They pack up the rest of their equipment and head for the closest store on the list.

Some of the actions you may have to implement as a result of monitoring and correcting response plans include the following:

- Modify project planning activities.

- Reexamine project requirements.

- Change project scope.

- Rework completed portions of the project.

- Improve change management procedures.

- Revise project schedule.

- Modify project budget.

- Revise performance measures.

Contingencies

A part of our risk planning process included developing contingency plans and budgets for those risks with impacts that weren't significant enough to warrant a fully developed plan. But what if the contingency plan isn't enough? If the impacts of the risk event are greater than anticipated and the contingency budget or plan can't accommodate the risk, you'll need to develop a risk response strategy and plan to handle the risk.

NOTE Small projects often have short time frames, and as a result, stakeholders believe risk planning and contingency planning aren't needed. If a risk event does occur on a small project, it could ruin the project's chances for success if there isn't a method to deal with the risks. Contingencies are a great strategy for small projects for exactly that reason—the time frame is quick and the scope is small.

Remember that risk identification and analysis is an iterative process that occurs throughout the life of the project. You're miles ahead of other project managers if you take the time to plan for risks during the planning stage, and I applaud your efforts to do so. Don't stop there. It's later when the work is chugging along and deliverables are getting met that, all of a sudden, a risk you didn't think was a big deal has the potential to be a big deal. That's when the value of proactively monitoring your risk list, assumptions, and response plans comes into play.

Continue to reevaluate your risks, assumptions, probability and impact, and response plans as you progress through the project.

Implementing Response Plans

You've spent a considerable amount of time identifying and prioritizing risks and developing response plans for those with the highest probabilities and highest impact. Your risk plans relate to the goals of the project, and the project, likewise, relates to the strategic objectives of the organization. You've progressively elaborated your risk list and risk responses so that when a risk event does occur, you're ready and prepared to mitigate its impacts by putting the response plan into action.

One of the items the risk management plan should document is how you go about implementing response plans. Does the project manager implement them? Does the risk owner? For those responses that require capital or resources, how do the funds get released? How are the resources assigned? These are the types of questions and processes that you should address in the risk management plan so that when it comes time to implement a risk response, everyone isn't standing around scratching their heads asking, "Gee, we have a great plan, but how do we put it into action?"

The following list will give you an idea of the steps involved in implementing a risk response plan and how to outline the procedure in the risk management plan. It isn't nearly as complicated as the list makes it look. However, you want to have a plan in place so that everyone knows exactly what to do when the risk event occurs. Don't wait until you're in crisis mode to figure out how to implement the plan.

1. Risk owner notifies the project manager of the risk event or risk trigger.

2. Project manager and the risk owner together agree that the response plan should be put into action.

3. Response plans are reexamined so that you're assured the strategy successfully mitigates the risk and reduces the impacts while capitalizing on opportunities.

4. Depending on the severity of risk, or the risk score, you may want to call a meeting of the project team and stakeholders to review the risk event and response plan prior to implementing.

5. Approval processes for budget expenditures are put into action when appropriate (not all risk responses require money to implement).

6. Resources are assigned to the risk response plan.

7. Response plan is implemented.

8. Risk owner monitors the effectiveness of the response plan and reports status at weekly project meetings.

9. Risk owner and project manager document results of the risk event and the response plan for the benefit of future projects.

The following flowchart shows the process outlined in the previous list.

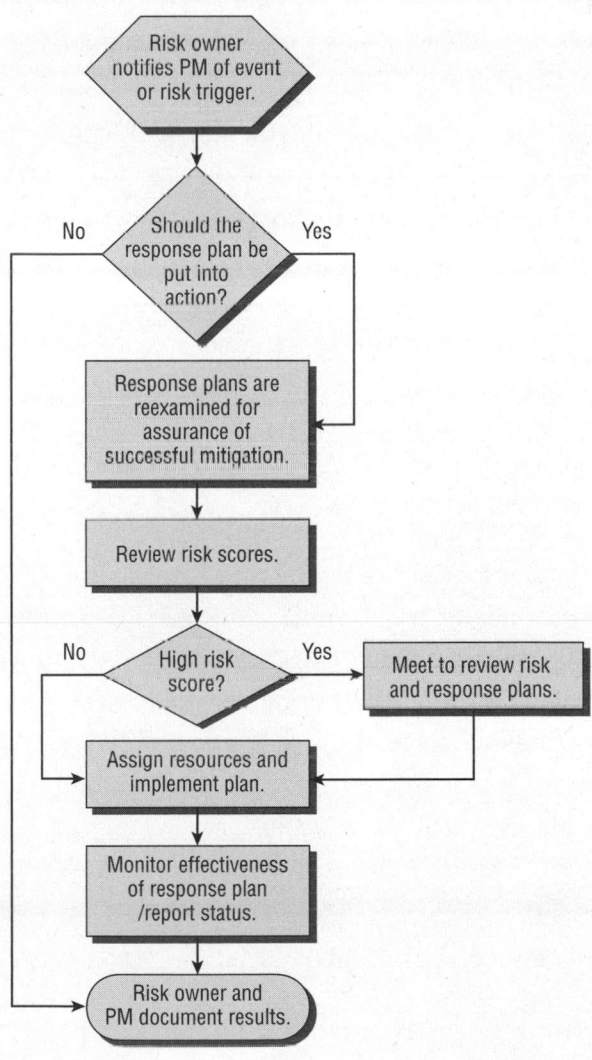

As mentioned in the previous list, once you put the response plans into action you'll want to monitor their effectiveness and regularly report on status and progress just as you do with the project plan. Track the amount of money spent on implementing the plan against the risk budget and the response plan estimates, and track and report on the actual number of resources required to mitigate the risk and the amount of time each resource spent on those tasks.

When to Implement

You'd probably agree that the answer to the "when to implement the plan?" question is self-evident—when the risk event occurs or a risk trigger signals that a risk is lurking around the corner and about to occur. After following the steps in the previous section and when you're certain the risk plan is valid, put it into action.

NOTE   I've talked about risk triggers several times throughout this book. Risk triggers warn you that risk event is about to occur. This is certainly one signal that means you should be prepared to put your plan into place.

And what about good old intuition? Have you ever had the feeling that you just know something is up? Don't ignore those feelings when it comes to project risk. Chances are you've subconsciously picked up clues along the way that are now jelling into that nagging gut feeling that something is amiss. Follow the Boy Scout model, and "be prepared." Review your risk list, talk to your project team, and keep honing in on that intuitive notion until you uncover some solid facts to back you up.

Unknown Risks

Unknown risks are those nasty critters that don't exist on your risk list and therefore have no response plans. So what happens when an unanticipated risk pops up? You implement a type of risk response plan called a *workaround*.

Workarounds are an unplanned response to a risk event that was unknown and unidentified during the risk identification process. They're also unplanned responses to risks that were previously accepted. You'll recall that the acceptance strategy says you'll deal with the risk and its impacts when and if it happens.

Workarounds are similar to contingency plans, only with contingency plans you think about a response before the risk happens. Workarounds are spur-of-the-moment responses. As such, they're usually more costly than risk response plans and can take more time to implement.

HEAVENLY THERAPY

Kevin and Li are partners who've recently opened a massage therapy center. One of the risks they identified in the planning stages of this project was building the clientele list. Their concern was that they wouldn't have enough folks booking massages to pay the bills during the first year of operation. They had a response plan in place to deal with this risk event; however, the exact opposite occurred. Their second month in operation found them with more clients than they could accommodate. This was an unplanned risk, and they decided to implement a workaround. They hired another therapist on contract to help with the overflow of customers while they formulated a better plan. This was costly in terms of money and time. They had to interview other massage therapists to find someone who shared their philosophies and practices, which took time. And they made little profit on the contractor's appointments. While they were able to book customers and keep them coming back for more (massages are addictive), they may have saved time and better capitalized on the opportunity this risk event presented if they had a response plan in place to deal with it.

Residual risks are often unknown risks. Residual risks are leftover risks, so to speak, from the original risk event or occur as a result of implementing the risk response plan. For example, Ned's project manager put into action the response plan to have the camera equipment shipped overnight after their café accident. This produced a residual risk because the camera supplier experienced a flooded basement the day before Sherry's call came in, which caused a delay in sending Ned's equipment.

While Sherry used good risk management practices, you can see that it didn't eliminate the possibility of risks occurring. Generally speaking, solid risk management principles will reduce the impacts of risk on the project to an acceptable tolerance level for your stakeholders. This doesn't mean you can kick back and think the risk plan will take care of all the risks. As you can see from this example, a residual risk occurred that wasn't identified in the planning stages.

Calling It Quits

One of the most difficult things to do as a project manager is to make the recommendation to kill a project. But when it's the right thing to do, you need to make the call.

Projects can succumb to an early demise for a number of reasons. Even good projects that are well planned, well managed, and have great risk management processes in place can still be plagued with too many change requests (or change requests that are so drastic they morph into a wholly different project), too many office politics, uninvolved project sponsors, and so on.

Many reasons may lead you to a kill recommendation. A few of them are as follows:

- Contingencies aren't sufficient to mitigate the risk event
- Vendor bankruptcy
- Excessive scope creep
- Changes in executive leadership

- Budget cuts

- Regulatory restrictions or changes

- Key technology isn't available or attainable

- Management and stakeholder turnover

- Market demands change

- New strategic or corporate strategies are implemented

- Competitors

- Project goes over the budget

- Unengaged project sponsor

- Poor project planning

- Limited availability of human resources

Be aware that stakeholders and project sponsors will use the reasoning that so much money has been invested to date on the project that they can't afford to call it quits. That just doesn't make logical sense. If the organization has made a mistake and the project isn't going to deliver what they thought it was going to deliver—whatever the reasons—should you continue to invest more time and money when you know it isn't going to get you where you need to go? No. It's time to admit that the project isn't going to meet the need, pull the plug, and stop the bleeding. Suppose you have a car that has been reliable over the years. It isn't a lot to look at, but it gets you from point A to point B. Suddenly, parts start going belly up, and the repair bills are higher than what a new car payment would be. Would you keep putting money into a car that's ten years old when you could pay the same or less for a newer, more reliable model? The same should hold true for your project.

NOTE   I've talked about gut feelings when it comes to risk before. Don't ignore those intuitive bursts of thought that tell you something isn't right.

Sometimes you as the project manager should consider passing on the opportunity to manage a project. Micromanagers, like I talked about in the previous chapter, are one of the reasons. Another is when the project sponsor insists that you must complete the project within a specific time frame and scope that you've already shown isn't possible. If the project estimates show that it isn't possible to complete the project and produce the level of quality it takes to satisfy the stakeholders, let the sponsor know you're moving on.

THE ACCOUNTING PROJECT

Ryan started his new job as project manager less than a month ago. He's responsible for three projects. One project continues to surface to the top of every conversation—the accounting project. The software the accounting group uses today performs well and meets the needs of the user community. The director of the accounting department insists they need a new software package that not only performs accounting functions but slices and dices too. After Ryan reexamines the requirements of the software package, he performs some financial analysis that shows the ongoing costs of the new system far exceed the costs of the existing system without additional benefit. He recommends the project be terminated.

Closing Out

As with everything else I've talked about, you'll want to document the results of the risk response plans. Some of the data you'll want to gather for this exercise can be addressed by asking the following questions regarding the risk response plans:

- Did the plan successfully mitigate the risk?

- Did the plan address all the risk, or did other events occur that were unplanned regarding this risk?

- Did you have to implement workarounds in addition to the response plans?

- Did the contingency plan adequately cover the contingencies?

This documentation comes in handy when you or another project manager begins work on a similar project in the future. The lessons learned on this project give project managers effective actions to take on future projects. If you have a list of risks, their responses, and the outcomes of those risks well documented, your next project's risk management process is already a step closer toward success.

Risk Audits

Risk audits are a method for examining the effectiveness of your risk management plan and risk response plans. It's a time to review what went well and not so well with the risk management processes. Taking the time to perform an audit at the end of your project provides several benefits, including assessing all of the following:

- Completeness of the risk management plan

- Success of the risk identification process

- Level of accuracy of probability and impact scores

- Performance of the risk owners

- Identification and monitoring of risk triggers

- Effectiveness of the risk response plans

- Risk budget

- Contingency plans

- Recommendations for future risk plans

Medium and large projects may have risk audits performed at major milestones throughout the project. Audits for small projects are easily performed at the end of the project. No matter the size of the project, remember to document the risks and their outcomes.

Risk audits, like lessons learned, aren't about finding fault with team members. No one will be honest with their assessments if they think you're going to use this information against them. Besides all that, if there were personnel issues along the way, you've waited way too long to deal with them if you're just now addressing them. You should deal with personnel issues when they occur, not at the end of the project.

NOTE   Make certain folks participating in the risk audit process know this isn't about assessing blame but rather is concerned with documenting what went well and recommending how to improve the processes for future projects.

Steps in a Risk Audit

Performing a risk audit isn't a complicated process. A few steps are involved, as with any process, but on a small-to-medium-sized project you should be able to complete most of these steps in one sitting.

Identify participants This one should be easy. The participants are likely the same folks who helped identify the risks, assisted with the response plans, and monitored the risk triggers and risk events throughout the project. You should also include the project sponsor and the key stakeholders because their perspective of the risk events may be different from the project team's perspective.

Conduct risk audit reviews Ask questions such as those outlined in the "Closing Out" section of this chapter. Examine the risk list and determine which of the risks occurred, determine which ones never surfaced, and identify risks that occurred that weren't recorded on the list. Ask your participants if the response plans were effective and, if not, what could have been done to make them more effective. The next section provides more detail on what questions to ask to assist the team with audit reviews.

Prepare recommendations After collecting the information, get with a few of your key team members to recommend how the risk management plan, risk identification, risk analysis, and risk response processes could be enhanced or improved. Determine what went well—because you'll want to repeat those elements on future projects—and determine what could be done better next time. Make certain you include specific recommendations on how to improve the processes next time. For example, perhaps not enough time was spent during project status review meetings to talk about risk status, so the recommendation should state that project meeting agendas should include time to review risk status.

Document the risk audit report In keeping with all good project management processes, document the risk audit process and the questions, answers, and recommendations, and file this with your lessons learned documentation on the project.

LESSONS LEARNED

Sean Jones wishes now he would have reviewed the lessons learned on a prior project that's similar in scope to the project he's managing. The previous project attempted to meet the same goals Sean's project is trying to accomplish. The risk audit report detailed the significant problems the team had with a particular key stakeholder and what they'd do differently. Unfortunately, Sean had to work with this same stakeholder on this project, and he repeated the mistakes the previous project manager made and ended up with the same fate. He's now looking for work.

Reviews

It may seem that all this review is more effort than it's worth. However, if your next project can benefit from even one thing you learn from performing this project, the effort will be worth it. Why continue to perpetuate bad processes or ineffective techniques? What you learn from this project will benefit others in your organization and will improve your performance as a project manager.

I've already mentioned some of the elements you should investigate during your risk audit. The following is a more complete list of questions to ask to help assess the effectiveness of your risk processes:

- Were the response plans implemented as written?

- Were all the revised plans documented?

- Did the response plans satisfactorily mitigate or reduce the impact of the risk event?

- Were the mitigation strategies chosen (avoidance, transfer, acceptance, mitigation) appropriate?

- Was the project managed using solid project management techniques?

- Were the appropriate personnel assigned as risk owners?

- Were the risk owners effective at informing the project manager when risks were about to occur?

- Did the risk owners implement the response plans at the right time?

- Did the risk owners monitor the response plans and recommend changes or modifications when needed?

- Did the risk triggers identified effectively signal risk events?

- Were there triggers that occurred that weren't recognized as triggers at the time?

- Did new risks present themselves?

- Was the contingency budget enough to cover risk expenses?

- Was the team effective at identifying risks?

- Should others have been interviewed or included in the risk identification and response planning sessions?

- Was the team effective at determining probability and impact?

- How many workarounds were put into place?

- How many unknown risks with unknown outcomes could have been identified earlier?

Case Study

Emily Lewis understands the importance of monitoring the project and the project environment for risk triggers and risk events. Emily knows the sooner the team responds to a risk event, the more likely they'll be able to reduce the impact of the risk event.

A few team meetings ago, a new risk was added to the risk list and a response plan was prepared. The risk was subcontractor failure. The vendor working on the CRM implementation outsourced the programming services to help keep the project on track. As the risk response predicted, the subcontractor failed to perform according to the contract standards.

Maria was assigned the owner of this risk. She works in the procurement area. However, it was actually a project team member who alerted Maria and Emily to the risk trigger. When the team member asked the vendor to provide the specifics of one of the database tables, the vendor couldn't provide the answer. The team member knew that the database table should have already been created and told Maria and Emily.

Emily contacted the primary vendor and insisted that they track down exactly where the subcontractor was according to the project schedule. Unfortunately, the subcontractor wasn't on track.

Maria and Emily together determined that the risk response plan should be put into action. They required the primary vendor to hire another subcontractor and insisted that the subcontractors work on location. This caused a residual risk because the additional contractors required space to perform their work at Emily's company. Although they brought their own laptops and cell phones, they still needed desks and chairs somewhere in close proximity to the rest of the team.

Requiring the subcontractor to work on-site was an addition to the original response plan that turned out to be extremely successful. The project team was able to monitor the work of the subcontractor and had a much better understanding of the amount of work completed to date than what they received via the vendor's status report.

The project proceeded from there according to plan and enjoyed a successful implementation. Emily took the time to perform a risk audit and review with her team members and key stakeholders. She documented the risk events that occurred, the effectiveness of the response plans, and the suggestions for improvements. She also documented the contingencies, workarounds, and changes to response plans—such as the previous one—that were put into place. No unidentified risks occurred during the project, and the team concluded it had done a fairly decent job of identifying, analyzing, monitoring, and implementing risk processes.

As Emily and team were celebrating the project success at a pizza party, Bill, the project sponsor, walked over and tapped her on the elbow.

"Great job, Emily. I'm thrilled with the success of this project."

"Thank you. I had a great team of folks to work with, and this project wouldn't have been a success without them."

"Ah, that's good to hear. Now for my question. The executive team has decided to upgrade the PBX system. I know the CRM system interfaces with the PBX; after all, you can't take a customer call without a telephone," he chuckles. "I'd like for you to head up this project. Are you interested?"

Emily, armed with the lessons learned and risk audit reviews from the CRM project, knows the answer without thinking. "Absolutely."

Nine Knowledge Areas Refresher

This appendix is a crash course on *A Guide to the PMBOK*'s project management process groups and the nine knowledge areas. All projects progress through a logical series of steps, starting with the initiation of a project all the way through to the ending, or closing, of the project. The information in this appendix will describe each of these processes along with the types of results or outcomes you're likely to see from each.

Following the process groups discussion, you'll find the nine knowledge areas. These describe the types of information and knowledge project managers must have to successfully run projects. Each knowledge area lists the project management processes found within that discipline, according to the 2000 and 2004 versions of *A Guide to the PMBOK*. Every four years, the Project Management Institute (PMI) modifies and enhances *A Guide to the PMBOK*. Changes reflect new information, industry trends, and best practices. Since the Spotlight Series spans both the 2000 and 2004 versions, you'll find both process listings in this appendix.

Project Management Process Groups

A Guide to the PMBOK describes and organizes the work of a project into five process groups: Initiating, Planning, Executing, Monitoring and Controlling, and Closing. Each group is interrelated and depends on the other. For example, you can't start the work of the project (Executing) without first initiating the project and creating a project plan—unless, of course, you work in Information Technology (IT) where we like to program the new system before we ask for requirements and then wonder why the end user doesn't like what we've done. (I trust all you great project managers out there are changing this paradigm.)

These process groups are iterative, meaning you might make several passes through each one throughout the course of the project. For example, changes might occur as a result of measurements you've taken (during the Monitoring and Controlling process) that require you go back to the Planning process and rework the schedule of some other part of the project plan. Risk management is iterative as well and should be performed throughout the life of the project.

Initiating

Initiating is the beginning process for all projects. This is where you decide whether to undertake the project by examining the costs and benefits of the project to the organization. It may also include an analysis of one project versus another project. For example, should you research and market a new product or consolidate the offices so all employees work under one roof? In the end, the Initiating process results in one of two decisions for each project considered—go or no go. Provided the answer is go, resources are committed to the project.

NOTE   Initiation is the formal recognition that a project, or the next phase in an existing project, should begin.

Some of the results produced during the Initiating process include the following:

- Defining the goals and objectives of the project
- Evaluating and determining project benefits
- Selecting projects based on criteria defined by a selection committee
- Writing the project charter
- Assigning the project manager
- Obtaining sign-off of the project charter

Planning

The Planning processes are the heart of all successful projects. And proper planning techniques can be the difference between a failed project and a successful one. This process outlines what's involved in completing the work of the project, where you're going, and how you're going to get there. As you probably already know, this process can consume a large amount of the overall project time, but it's well worth the investment.

Project planning involves researching, communicating, and documenting—and lots of it. What you do here will determine how the project will progress through the remaining processes. It also establishes the foundation for the rest of the project. If you communicate well with the stakeholders through this process, assure that all project team members and stakeholders understand the purpose of the project and how the work will be carried out, and establish a professional decorum with everyone involved, the stakeholders will feel confident that the project will be successful. You're also more likely to gain their cooperation later in the project when the problems start to appear.

Some of the results produced during Planning include the following:

- Determining project deliverables and milestones

- Writing and publishing a scope statement

- Determining requirements

- Breaking down the work of the project into tasks and creating a Work Breakdown Structure (WBS)

- Developing a project schedule

- Establishing a project budget

- Developing risk, communication, quality, and change management plans

- Determining resource needs

- Assessing special skills needed for project tasks and identifying resources

- Setting the stage for project success

> **NOTE**   The Planning group is the largest of all the process groups. The project plans created here are the road map for achieving the goals the project was undertaken to address.

Executing

While the Planning process is the heart of determining project success, the Executing process is where the real work of the project actually happens. Great plans require follow-through, and this is what you do in the Executing process group.

In the Executing process you'll put all the project plans you've developed into action. Project team members complete the tasks. You keep the project team focused on the work of the project, and you communicate project progress to stakeholders and management. Once the work of the project begins, sometimes you'll need to change the project plan. It's the project manager's responsibility to update the project planning documents and redirect and refocus the project team on the correct tasks.

The Executing process is where you'll likely utilize the majority of project resources, spend most of the project budget, and run into scheduling conflicts.

Some of the results produced during the Executing process include the following:

- Obtaining project resources
- Establishing the project team
- Directing and leading the project team
- Conducting project status meetings
- Publishing project status reports and other project information
- Communicating project information
- Managing and directing contractors
- Managing project progress
- Implementing quality assurance procedures

Monitoring and Controlling

This group of project management processes involves monitoring the work of the project and taking performance measures to assure that the work performed is on track with the project scope and that the deliverables are being met. If performance checks during this process show that the project has veered off course, corrective action is required to realign the work of the project with the project goals.

Corrections and changes during this process may require a trip back through the Planning and Executing processes. Most often this will occur for one of two reasons—change requests or corrective actions.

Some of the results produced during the Monitoring and Controlling process include the following:

- Measuring performance and comparing to project plan

- Ensuring that the project progresses according to plan

- Taking corrective action when measures are outside limits

- Evaluating the effectiveness of corrective actions

- Reviewing and implementing change requests

- Updating the project plan to conform with change requests

Closing

The Closing process is the one project managers tend to skip. Once the project at hand is complete, it's easy to start focusing on the next one. Who wants to obtain sign-off, document lessons learned, and close out a project that's complete and that stakeholders love? You should.

One of the most important aspects of this process is documenting lessons learned. You and your project team have just completed a successful project where some processes worked very well and others could have been improved. Now is the time to capture the good and the bad so that the next project you (or another project manager in your company) undertake capitalizes on the lessons learned during this project.

Another aspect of this process is celebrating. Your team has met or exceeded the agreed-upon project goals, and the stakeholders are satisfied. That spells success, and success should be celebrated. Projects are truly team efforts, and it's always appropriate to congratulate your team on a job well done.

Some of the results produced during the Closing process include the following:

- Obtaining acceptance of project deliverables

- Securing sign-off from all stakeholders

- Documenting lessons learned

- Archiving project records

- Formalizing the closure of the project

- Releasing project resources

Figure A.1 shows the interaction and iterative nature of these process groups. While all the process groups are iterative, you'll find that most interaction occurs between the Planning, Executing, and Controlling process groups.

FIGURE A.1: Project process groups

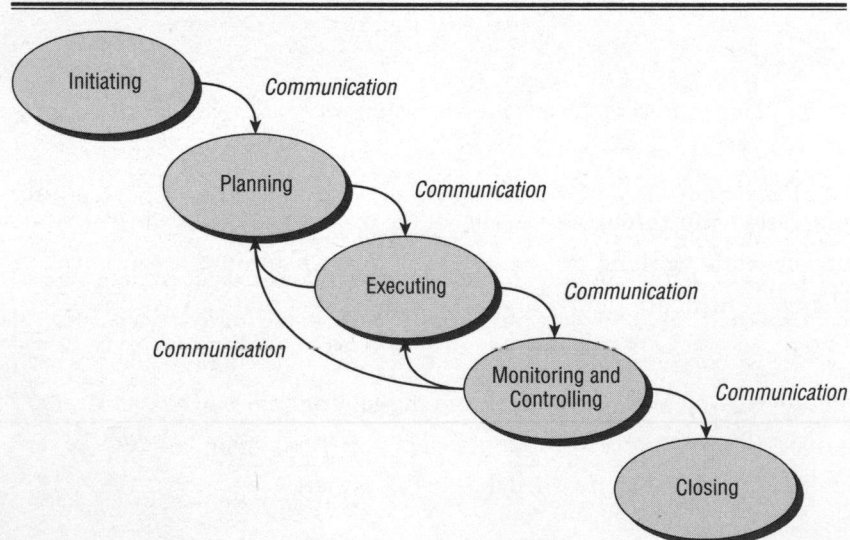

Project Management Knowledge Areas

According to *A Guide to the PMBOK*, nine knowledge areas comprise project management: Project Integration Management, Project Scope Management, Project Time Management, Project Cost Management, Project Quality Management, Project Human Resources Management, Project Communications Management, Project Risk Management, and Project Procurement Management. Each knowledge area deals with a specific aspect of project management such as scope management and time management. These areas consist of individual processes that have characteristics in common. For example, the Project Procurement Management knowledge area consists of processes dealing with procurement planning, solicitation, source selection, contract administration, and so on.

You should familiarize yourself with each knowledge area and the processes they include. They provide the foundation for solid project management practices.

If you'd like further information on these knowledge areas and their processes, pick up a copy of *PMP Project Management Professional Study Guide* by Kim Heldman.

The knowledge areas and a brief description of each follow.

Project Integration Management

The Project Integration Management knowledge area is concerned with coordinating all aspects of the project plan and is highly interactive. It involves project planning, project execution, and change control. All these processes occur throughout the life of the project and are repeated continuously while working on the project. Project planning, execution, and change control are tightly linked. The processes that constitute Project Integration Management include the following:

2000 PMBOK	2004 PMBOK
Project Plan Development	Develop Project Charter
Project Plan Execution	Develop Preliminary Project Scope

2000 PMBOK	2004 PMBOK
Integrated Change Control	Develop Project Management Plan
	Direct and Manage Project Execution
	Monitor and Control Project Work
	Integrated Change Control
	Close Project

Project Scope Management

The Project Scope Management knowledge area is concerned with defining all the work of the project and only the work required to complete the project. The processes involved in project scope management occur at least once during the life of the project and sometimes many times throughout the life of the project. For instance, Scope Planning entails defining and documenting the work of the project. Scope Change Control is the process that handles changes to the agreed-upon scope. Changes, as you probably guessed, require changes to the Scope Planning process, and thus the cycle perpetuates. The processes that constitute Project Scope Management include the following:

2000 PMBOK	2004 PMBOK
Initiation	Scope Planning
Scope Planning	Scope Definition
Scope Definition	Create WBS
Scope Verification	Scope Verification
Scope Change Control	Scope Control

Project Time Management

The Project Time Management knowledge area is concerned with setting the duration of the project plan activities, devising a project schedule, and monitoring and controlling deviations from the schedule. Time management is an important aspect of project management because it keeps the project activities on track and monitors those activities against the project plan to ensure the project is completed on time. The processes that constitute Project Time Management include the following:

2000 PMBOK	2004 PMBOK
Activity Definition	Activity Definition
Activity Sequencing	Activity Sequencing
Activity Duration Estimating	Activity Resource Estimating
Schedule Development	Activity Duration Estimating
Schedule Control	Schedule Development
	Schedule Control

Project Cost Management

As its name implies, the Project Cost Management knowledge area involves project costs and budgets. The activities in the Project Cost Management area establish estimates for costs and resources and keep watch over those costs to ensure that the project stays within the approved budget. The processes that make up Project Cost Management include the following:

2000 PMBOK	2004 PMBOK
Resource Planning	Cost Estimating
Cost Estimating	Cost Budgeting
Cost Budgeting	Cost Control
Cost Control	

Project Quality Management

Project Quality Management ensures that the project meets the requirements that the project was undertaken to produce. It focuses on product quality as well as the quality of the project management processes used during the project's life cycle. The processes in this knowledge area measure overall performance, monitor project results, and compare them to the quality standards. All this means the customer will receive the product or service they thought they purchased. The processes that constitute Project Quality Management include the following:

2000 PMBOK	2004 PMBOK
Quality Planning	Quality Planning
Quality Assurance	Perform Quality Assurance
Quality Control	Perform Quality Control

Project Human Resource Management

Ah, the people factor. Project activities don't perform themselves. It takes a village…no, that's someone else's line. It takes people to perform the activities of a project. The Project Human Resource Management knowledge area assures that the human resources assigned to the project are used in the most effective way possible. Some of the skills covered in this knowledge area include personal interaction, leading, coaching, conflict management, performance appraisals, and so on. The processes that constitute Project Human Resource Management include the following:

2000 PMBOK	2004 PMBOK
Organizational Planning	Human Resource Planning
Staff Acquisition	Acquire Project Team
Team Development	Develop Project Team
	Manage Project Team

Project Communications Management

The processes in this knowledge area are related to—you guessed it—communication skills. Communication encompasses much more than just a simple exchange of information. The Project Communications Management knowledge area ensures that all project information—including project plans, risk assessments, risk response plans, meeting notes, project status, and more—are collected, documented, distributed, and archived at appropriate times. Project managers use communication skills on a daily basis. According to some statistics (and most of you can attest to this from first-hand experience), project managers spend 90 percent of their time communicating. The processes that constitute Project Communications Management include the following:

2000 PMBOK	2004 PMBOK
Communication Planning	Communications Planning
Information Distribution	Information Distribution
Performance Reporting	Performance Reporting
Administrative Closure	Manage Stakeholders

Project Risk Management

The Project Risk Management knowledge area deals with identifying, analyzing, and planning for potential risks. This includes minimizing the likelihood of risk events occurring, minimizing risk consequences, and exploiting positive risks that may improve project performance or outcomes. The processes that constitute Project Risk Management include the following:

2000 PMBOK	2004 PMBOK
Risk Management Planning	Risk Management Planning
Risk Identification	Risk Identification
Qualitative Risk Analysis	Qualitative Risk Analysis
Quantitative Risk Analysis	Quantitative Risk Analysis
Risk Response Planning	Risk Response Planning
Risk Monitoring and Control	Risk Monitoring and Control

Project Procurement Management

The Project Procurement Management knowledge area concerns the purchasing of goods or services from external vendors, contractors, and suppliers. These processes deal with preparing requests for information from contractors, evaluating responses, and selecting the contractor to perform the work or supply the goods. It also deals with contract administration and contract closeout. The processes that constitute Project Procurement Management include the following:

2000 PMBOK	2004 PMBOK
Procurement Planning	Plan Purchases and Acquisitions
Solicitation Planning	Plan Contracting
Solicitation	Request Seller Responses
Source Selection	Select Sellers
Contract Administration	Contract Administration
Contract Closeout	Contract Closure

Risk Management Templates

Your life as a project manager can be quite challenging at times. As you perfect your skills you find tools and techniques that work for you. You incorporate them into your project manager tool belt for use on your next project. I have provided here a set of templates for your future use. You've also find them located at www.harborlightpress.com or www.sybex.com. I hope you find them to be great additions to your project management tool belt.

Checklist of Common Risks

I. General Information

Project name:_____   Project number:_____

Project manager name: _____   Date:_____

II. Checklist

CATEGORY OF RISK	RISK	EXAMINED
Personnel	Loss of key employee	☐
	Low availability of qualified personnel	☐
	Inadequate skills and training	☐
Project management	Inadequate skills and ability of the project manager	☐
	Inadequate skills and ability of business users or subject matter experts	☐
	Inadequate skills and ability of vendors	☐
	Poor project management processes	☐
	Lack of, or poorly designed, change management processes	☐
	Lack of, or poorly designed, risk management processes clearly defined	☐
Financial	Inadequate project budgets	☐
	Cost overruns	☐
	Funding cuts	☐
	Unrealistic or inaccurate cost estimates	☐
Organizational/business	Lack of stakeholder consensus	☐
	Changes in key stakeholders	☐
	Lack of involvement by project sponsor	☐
	Loss of project sponsor during the project	☐
	Changes in company ownership	☐
	Organizational structure	☐
Business	Changing market demands	☐
	Competitor activities	☐
	Poor timing of product releases	☐
	Unavailability of resources and materials	☐
	Poor public image	☐
External	Environmental threats	☐
	Uncooperative weather conditions	☐
	Civil unrest	☐
	Labor strikes or work stoppages	☐
	Seasonal or cyclical events	☐
	Lack of vendor and supplier availability	☐
	Financial instability of vendors and suppliers	☐
Technical	Complex technology	☐
	New or unproven technology	☐
	Availability of technology	☐
Performance	Unrealistic performance goals	☐
	Immeasurable performance standards	☐
Cultural	Resistance to change	☐
	Cultural barriers (diversity, corporate culture, international projects)	☐
Internal	Unavailability of business experts	☐
	Unavailability of technical experts	☐
Scope	Unrealistic or incomplete scope definition	☐
	Scope statement not agreed to by all stakeholders	☐
Schedule	Unrealistic or incomplete schedule development	☐
	Unrealistic or incomplete activity estimates	☐
Quality	Unrealistic quality objectives	☐
	Not meeting quality standards	☐

Risk Identification Checklist

I. General Information

Project name:_____ Project number:_____

Project manager name: _____ Date:_____

II. Checklist

ACTION ITEM	DESCRIPTION	COMPLETED
Examine historical information.	Review project planning documents and prior projects that are similar in scope and complexity to the current project.	☐
Review constraints.	Constraints restrict or dictate the actions of the project team and may have inherent risks associated with them.	☐
Perform assumptions analysis.	Review assumptions for validity.	☐
Determine risk categories.	Create risk categories, or use organization- or industry-defined categories.	☐
Perform information-gathering techniques.	Determine the best method for identifying risks, and conduct the process.	☐
Document risks.	Document risks with an unique ID number, category, risk name, and description number.	☐

Risk List

I. General Information

Project name:_____   Project number:_____

Project manager name: _____   Date:_____

II. Project Overview   *Describe the goals and the purpose of the project.*

III. Risk List   *List identified risks.*

ID	Risk	Description	Probability	Impact	Risk Score	Owner

Risk Management Plan

I. General Information

Project name:_____   Project number:_____

Project manager name: _____   Date:_____

II. Project Overview   *Describe the goals and the purpose of the project.*

III. Methodology   *Describe the processes used for identifying and documenting risks.*

Risk identification methodology:
Prioritization methodology:
Method for development of risk response plans:
Method for monitoring risk response plans and triggers:

IV. Roles and Responsibilities   *Describe the roles and responsibilities of risk reporters, owners, and the project manager.*

Project manager:
Risk reporters:
Risk owners:
Project sponsor:
Other stakeholders:

V. Budget   *Describe the risk management budget.*

Budget amount for risks:
Budget amount for contingencies:

VI. Reporting Formats   *Describe the mechanism for reporting risks.*

Location of risk documents:
Risk identification reports:
    Frequency:
Risk response plan reports:
    Frequency:
Risk status reporting method:
    Frequency:

Risk Response Plan

I. General Information

Project name:_____ Project number:_____

Project manager name: _____ Date:_____

II. Risk Information   *Describe the risk-tracking information.*

Risk ID:_____ Risk owner:_____

Probability:_____ Risk originator:_____

Impact:_____ Expected value:_____

III. Response Plan   *Describe the risk response plan.*

Risk description:

Impact and consequences:

Additional information:

Risk triggers:

Response plan:

Resources need to implement the plan:

Risk Submission Form

I. General Information

Project name:_____   Project number:_____

Project manager name: _____   Date:_____

II. Risk Originator   *Identify the risk originator.*

Originator name:_____

Phone number:_____

E-mail:_____

III. Risk Description   *Describe the risk and its impacts.*

Risk name:

Description:

Potential impact:

    Business unit:

    Customers:

    Cost:

    Schedule:

    Scope:

    Other:

Glossary

acceptance
A risk response strategy that accepts the consequences of a risk event should it occur.

accountability
Assuring that the project is completed to the satisfaction of the stakeholders, on time, and within budget.

assumptions
Events or actions believed to be true. Risk assumptions should always be documented.

authority
The ability to make and enforce decisions and to administer consequences and rewards to team members.

avoidance
A risk response strategy that attempts to avoid or eliminate risk events and their impacts.

cardinal scale values
Values expressed as numbers between 0 and 1.0 and referenced in the Qualitative Risk Analysis process.

constraints
Actions or decisions that either restrict or dictate the actions of the project team.

contingency planning

A risk response strategy that involves planning alternatives to deal with the risks should they occur.

contingency reserves

Contingency reserves hold project funds, time, or resources in reserve to offset any unavoidable threats that might occur to project scope, schedule, cost overruns, or quality.

critical success factors

Those elements that must be completed in order for the project to be considered complete.

decision tree analysis

A diagramming method that shows the sequence of interrelated decisions and the expected results of choosing one alternative over another. It's usually used for risk events that impact time or cost.

expected value

An overall risk score derived by multiplying the risk impact value by the risk probability value.

force majeure

Catastrophic risks that are outside the scope of risk management planning such as earthquakes, meteorites, volcanoes, floods, civil unrest, and terrorism.

impact

The consequences of a risk event. This is how the risk will affect the project should it be realized.

influence

The ability to get people to do things they wouldn't ordinarily do without the use of force or coercion.

mitigation
A proactive risk response strategy that reduces the probability of a risk event and its impacts to an acceptable level.

Monte Carlo analysis
A statistical technique that uses simulation to calculate a distribution of probable results.

ordinal values
Rank-ordered values such as High, Medium, and Low. They're used during the Qualitative Risk Analysis process to assign risk scores to identified risks.

probability
The likelihood that a risk event will occur.

project charter
An official, written acknowledgment and recognition that a project exists. The charter gives the project manager the authority to assign organizational resources to the work of the project.

Qualitative Risk Analysis
This process determines what impact the identified risks will have on the project and the probability they'll occur. Rank orders risks in priority order according to their effect on the project objectives.

Quantitative Risk Analysis
This process assigns numeric probabilities to each identified risk and examines its potential impact on the project objectives.

residual risk
A risk that remains or is the result of implementing a risk response strategy.

risk
An event that poses a threat or an opportunity to the project.

risk audit

A method for examining the effectiveness of the risk management plan and risk processes.

risk identification

This process identifies the potential project risks and documents their characteristics.

risk management

Applying skills, knowledge, and risk management tools and techniques to the project in order to reduce threats to an acceptable level while maximizing opportunities.

risk management plan

Details how the risk management processes will be implemented, monitored, and controlled throughout the life of the project.

risk monitoring

An activity that includes gathering information, documenting the findings, and reporting the findings.

Risk Monitoring and Control

This process responds to risks as they occur, tracks and monitors identified risks, evaluates risk response plans for effectiveness, identifies new risks, and ensures that proper risk management procedures are followed as defined in the risk management plan.

risk originator

Team members, stakeholders, or others who identify a potential risk and inform the project manager.

risk owner

The team member responsible for managing an identified risk by tracking risk activities, monitoring the project and other events for risk triggers, carrying out the risk response plan, and monitoring the effectiveness of the response plan.

risk response plan

The risk response plan details how risk response strategies will be implemented when the risk event occurs.

risk response planning

This process defines what steps to take to reduce threats and take advantage of opportunities. Assigns departments or individuals the responsibility of carrying out risk response plans.

risk tolerance

The level of risk an organization or individual is willing to accept.

risk trigger

Symptoms of a risk that imply a risk event is about to occur.

sensitivity analysis

A modeling technique that determines which risk event has the greatest potential for impact. It examines the extent to which the uncertainty of a risk event affects the project objectives.

simulation techniques

Analysis techniques that use various assumptions to calculate a distribution of probable results.

transference

A risk response strategy that transfers the consequences of a risk to a third party. Insurance is an example of transference.

Work Breakdown Structure (WBS)

A deliverables-oriented hierarchy that defines the total work of the project. Each WBS level has more detailed information than the previous level.

workaround

An unplanned response to an unknown, unidentified risk or a previously accepted risk.

Index

Note to the Reader: Throughout this index **boldfaced** page numbers indicate primary discussions of a topic. *Italicized* page numbers indicate illustrations.

Project Manager's Spotlight Series

The Project Manager's Spotlight series highlights critical components of the project management process and offers clear and concise coverage that is more accessible and applicable than general management titles on the market. The Spotlight Series is written for project managers, team leaders, and team members involved with small-to medium-sized projects on short schedules who are seeking fast, practical solutions to risk management, change management, and/or project planning.

Project Manager's Spotlight on Risk Management

By Kim Heldman, PMP
ISBN: 0-7821-4411-X

Project Manager's Spotlight on Change Management

By Claudia Baca, PMP
ISBN: 0-7821-4410-1

Project Manager's Spotlight on Planning

By Catherine A. Tomczyk, PMP
ISBN: 0-7821-4413-6

To place an order call 1-800-956-7739
or visit us at www.josseybass.com.

JOSSEY-BASS